Overcoming Evil

”Love opens our eyes, shows us the truth and
allows us to perceive truth in all things.”

PEKKA ERVAST

Overcoming Evil

Pekka Ervast Series IV

ESPOO

2024

Table of contents:

For the reader   7

I
Bodhisattva, Buddha, and Christ   9

II
The phases of the life of Satan   25

III
Do demons exist?   37

IV
The Eternal Fight   53

V
Will Light Win?   69

VI
Lucifer and Antichrist   85

VII
By whose help – our own?   97

VIII
The Antichrist   115

IX
How does Christ help us?   127

X
Love   147

XI
Love one another   155

Publications in English:

The Mission of the Theosophical Society, An open letter to Theosophists the world over (1921)

The Sermon on the Mount, or the Key to Christianity (1933)

"H. P. B."; Four Episodes from the Life of the Sphinx of the Nineteenth Century (1933)

The Esoteric School of Jesus (1979)

Astral Schools (ebook 1979)

The Key to the Kalevala (1999)

The Divine Seed: The Esoteric Teachings of Jesus (2010)

From Death to Rebirth (ebook 2017)

From Death to Rebirth (audiobook 2018)

Spiritual Knowledge (2018)

The Inner God and Happiness (2018)

The Inner God and Happiness (ebook 2018)

The Unseen Ecclesia (2021)

Esoteric Schools and the Occult World (2024)
Talk by Pekka Ervast
(hermesrisen.wordpress.com)

Pekka Ervast's Talk to the Esotericists (2024)
(www.theosophyforward.com)

The Hidden Life of Christianity: The Elemental of Faith
(hermesrisen.wordpress.com)

Overcoming Evil (2024)

www.pekkaervast.net

The author of the book is Pekka Ervast (1875-1934), Founder and General Secretary of the Finnish section of The Theosophical Society, Founder-President of the Finnish Rosicrucian Society, 33 degree founder-member of the Finnish section of the International Order of Freemasonry Le Droit Humain. Founder-President and Grand Master of the Finnish Rosicrucian Freemasonry.

The public lectures in this book were given by Pekka Ervast in Helsinki in the spring-winter of 1930. They were written in shorthand and published as a book after Ervast's death only in 1964. They are still important for those of us who want to understand the origin and purpose of evil.

To solve the mystery of evil, we need to understand the history of human evolution, which theosophical research has opened up for us Westerners. Humanity today is already on the 4th day of creation, each of which has lasted millions of years. During the root races of the current creation day, we have evolved both externally and internally from animal-like unconscious beings to modern human beings who critically examine life. Ignorance has led humans to act selfishly as self-interested or imitating and following others. Therein lies the origin of evil. We do not always realise that so-called evil is the result of our own choices.

Fortunately, we have not been left to our own luck, but as early as Lemuria, the 3rd root race, saviour beings from other planets came to Earth to teach our infant humanity. Through the teachings and reincarnations of established religions, we have learned to be more thoughtful and understanding.

Now we each have the opportunity to understand how to overcome the temporal evil within ourselves. And the more of us who do so, the sooner the present humanity will enter its new phase of development.

Seppo Aalto

I

Bodhisattva, Buddha, and Christ

This planet of ours is sometimes called a small island in the vast sea of the world. Indeed, if we take a moment to observe our planet from the outside, from the perspective of our own Solar System, we see that it is a small island, a small wheel traveling along its trajectory in this unthinkably vast Solar System. In our Solar System, there are other planets traveling along their cyclic trajectories around our Earth, even though their trajectories follow definite orbits. We are accustomed to think each of these planets is some kind of a school for living beings. These different schools might even be for different kinds of beings, as the possibilities of life differ on different planets just from a physiological perspective. The beings living on those other planets are different from us and from each other and on different stages of evolution. It is of no use for us to think about the conditions on different planets; it is enough for us to get a truer understanding of what they are like on our own planet. We are called upon to investigate this subject, and not only to investigate it but to vividly resolve it.

When we compare those other planet schools to our own, we notice, as Madame Blavatsky stated in the Secret

Doctrine, that our planet is at that age and that stage of evolution where the human being is born. All high beings have always passed through the human stage, which is a very critical stage in evolution. Therefore, the planet dedicated to human life and the birth and evolution of mankind, is one of the most important planets in the Solar System. At this stage, the planet is then also at a critical and difficult stage of its own evolution. As the wise ones say, in all evolution the human stage is so important and so difficult because only this stage will give birth to a new god, an individual destined to become a divine being. This process of individualization, followed by evolution as a human, is so difficult and dangerous, for it is not only some natural process of evolution happening by itself but a peculiar process of ethical evolution, in which the individual in question must by themselves make the choice between good and evil. In order for the individual to learn to be good in a true sense, freely good – a divine being who has chosen good and wants to serve good from their own inner conviction – they must be able to make this choice of their own free conviction. It is not enough for the gods in the universe to be such beings who do not understand why they want to do good or why they have chosen good. The human stage is so peculiar because the individual is placed in this critical school and faced with the choice between good and evil. It is a separate matter whether the individual chooses good and chooses it promptly. However, behind this question there are enormous inner pains and sufferings, a process of overcoming oneself, for the critical and difficult aspect lies in the evil that draws the individuality towards itself at an unlimited strength. Selfishness is more tempting in the beginning of the human stage than unselfishness, and the individual must go through many phases before they can choose good. This planet is called the school of painful endeavors, because it is where the creation of human beings unfolds. A human is born, and is asked: Do you want to create a human?

How is this possible, and how can this happen? If we try, in our imagination, to look at this matter from the outside, with Earth before our eyes, we will see how Earth is given in the dawning of time to the care of a great and beautiful being of light. To this wondrously high and wise being of light is entrusted the difficult school of Earth. It is painful and difficult even for this planetary spirit, the guiding being, because he must cover himself, totally conceal himself, to be off the stage and only let loose in this school the wonderful, high, and good creative power. The mystery of the creative power is set loose in this school, on this planet. We understand that there cannot be good without evil or impurity without sanctity, just like how counterfeit money cannot exist without real money. There must first be real money, and only after it can there be false money. There must first be good, and only then evil. First good and pure, only then can there be unclean, unpure, and unholy. The creative power that this wonderful being of light unleashes in this school on our Earth is a double-edged sword because it is both the creative power in the partially material sense, i.e., the power to procreate, but also the internal creative power; the creative power of spirit and reason, the power of imagination. It is the sexual power, but it is also the Holy Spirit itself. It is the creative power of the Holy Spirit in the innermost chamber of Earth, generated within this being of light and radiating out of him. Thus, humans are the beings in which, after a long evolution, the self is born. This human self then ends up in a struggle with the powers of nature.

The self is given the strangest power of all; the power to procreate, the creative power of spirit. As a small self, as an infant soul, the human being must contend with the mysterious, grand powers of life.

This power living within man is also double-edged in the sense that it creates pleasure and suffering through feelings and sensations. It follows that the general opposites in nature and life become clear to the being developing towards thought. In this school of humans, the opposites are beginning to show: good in that which creates pleasure, evil in that which causes suffering. These are the primary opposites. While human beings become more and more civilized and moral, their original sensations focus on their own personal human form.

Should humanity be left alone to eat from the tree of the knowledge of good and evil, we would have no guarantees of how long it would take before individual humans, divine individuals, would emerge from humanity. Who knows if these little human individuals would end up astray, away from God, and be subjugated to pleasures, seeking only pleasure. Therefore, it is not so in life, and not in our Solar System either, that this planet, given as a school for the birth and evolution of the human self, would be left on its own. That would be like a country ruled by total anarchy: a country with only a few individuals thinking about anything else but themselves and their lives. They would have no guidance for eons until someone with both power and intellect emerged. However, that individual would most likely be evil, as there would not be much knowledge about good in the beginning. Therefore, our planet has not been left on its own, which is not customary in the life of the universe. The great economy of the universe is arranged in a way where the older ones take care of the younger ones. Parents feel obliged to take care of their child. When our planet was young, when mankind had just been born on it, help was ordered for it from somewhere else, as we have always reiterated. Help came here from another star, from a planet with more evolved human beings. Here, I do not just mean that those beings were externally similar to us, but that they were humans in the sense that they had resolved the question of good and evil, choosing good, and had thus solved the problem of the human, creating the perfect human. A few such beings and their aides had received an order to relocate to our planet, to be our leaders and protectors here, providing support to a small, newborn human. And so, they moved here.

The Old Testament, revered by Christians as a valuable and sacred book, refers to this when it speaks of Melchizedek, the king of Salem and the great king of peace, who came here along with his group of allies. As is said of Melchizedek, he had neither a father nor a mother. He was a very peculiar king in the Old Testament, spoken of in connection with Abraham. Melchizedek blessed Abraham and received tithes from the spoils of war, from Abraham's military campaign. Not much else is told about him in the Old Testament, but the New Testament tells us that Jesus Christ is the highest priest after the order of Melchizedek. The text suggests that Melchizedek had a school or university of some kind where Jesus Christ acquired the qualifications to become the highest priest.

This name "Melchizedek" refers to that Secret Brotherhood which came from elsewhere, establishing the human, divine academy here. The Brotherhood oversees the spiritual life of humanity as its teacher. Melchizedek and his group came here to support and teach humanity. They came here to show human beings the way: how to eat from the tree of the knowledge of good and evil, how to act and behave, so that they could choose what is right and good. They came to show people how they could reach the human goal: eternal life. This is what they came here to teach.

Now we know that our eternal life is in the cosmic life we call Christ. We could say that Melchizedek and his academy came to teach us how we could find the Cosmic Christ, how we could participate in the spiritual life available to people, which strives to reach humanity, to vivify it, and to raise it to eternal immortality. Naturally, Melchizedek and his aides all lived in Christ. If we think of Christ as the tree of life – a term used in ancient scriptures to describe this cosmic, mystical life – Melchizedek and his fellows brought a branch of the tree of life, the Banyan tree, and planted it when they established the divine academy here. However, we cannot state that they brought the tree of life itself. They themselves lived in the tree of life, without being able to bring it to Earth in totality. Why could they not? For the simple reason that they came from elsewhere. We can understand this through metaphor: let us imagine that here on our planet some nation was living in anarchy, perhaps in a war among themselves and without a leader. Then a civilized nation would send them a group of people to raise them and teach them – let us not think about beings like us, neither generals nor troops of war – a wise one and his aides would come to this nation to teach and advise them, to show an example and provide good knowledge and skills. The wise one and his fellows would form a society for them. Then they would naturally teach and enlighten those human beings to a great extent. However, even if the outsiders had learned the language of the local people, they would not be able to fully help them. This is because they are not from the same family or tribe, and they had not grown up in these circumstances to truly understand the soul of this community, including every individual separately.

This example is clumsy, but we chose it thinking of the natural conditions of how hard it would be for us to understand other nations and cultures. If we imagine that those locals were black, and we, the wise ones helping them, were white, we would find it difficult to fully understand them and to gain their trust, even after having taught them. We would not be able to penetrate their souls before they themselves would begin to understand themselves and to bring out what is inside of them.

If we were to say, considering Earth and the conditions herein, that the Cosmic Christ Himself had to be planted here as the tree of life – not merely as a branch of the tree – we would understand that Christ had to manifest by being born through a denizen of this Earth. His arrival is not through teachings; rather, He must be born on this planet. He does not come here through someone merely talking about Him, showing that Christ is in him, but by one person after another receiving a little of this Christ over the course of millions of years, until eventually someone can fully embrace Him and plant the tree of life in the herb garden of this life.

Looking from this point of view, we understand the relation of the Secret Brotherhood to our planet, to humanity, and then to the Cosmic Christ. Melchizedek and his aides were like professors who came here from somewhere else and established a university here, telling us what kinds of examinations we must pass to get degrees in this university, at the same time teaching us how we must acquire this knowledge. To me personally, this metaphor of an academy and professors is very accurate, even though this academy and its professors are much higher than the universities of this world. The one who came from elsewhere is such a high headmaster that without his permission, no one can become anything. No one can get any degrees unless he permits it, unless he lets his star shine. Such is the order of things. Naturally, many individuals, one after another, became infatuated with these teachers and helpers and all that they were shown in images and visions. This was at the time when language was still poor, and in this fifth root-race, in which intellect is more evolved than before, both linguistically and philosophically. Naturally, people, one after another, got excited and began to understand that they are in a wonderful school. They realized that they must not selfishly dive into pleasure and evil, but instead they must find an aspiration for which it is worth living and dying. More and more people on this planet and from our humanity received this aspiration and began to go forward, to raise themselves, to place their own power according to life's will and overcome the great selfishness to which they are drawn by this force of nature.

More and more people began to notice that this being behind our planet, keeping us in a tough school and anxiety, appears to us disguised, so that we do not know whether he is anything else but this mask. This being first incites us into evil, saying, "You are a child of the world; you must make a living in this life. You must think about your own happiness and strive for pleasure, wealth, and power." Such a great temptation, a compelling force of nature, lives within a human being. It is not as easy as it seems to us in our great moments to give up all selfishness, which is so close to us. We are relatively undeveloped yet, or hypocritical, if we think we can give up selfishness just like that. In reality, this is very difficult, for that temptation lives within us, trying to force us into selfishness and pleasure. Therefore, this self-education, which all great teachers have required from human beings since the dawn of time, feels overwhelming and almost impossible. It feels so impossible that the individual shouts nearly powerless, "It cannot be that I have to give up happiness and myself!" But the great teachers have always calmly stated, "Rise, awaken and seek teachers!" Thus echoes the shout telling us, the fifth root-race, that an individual can overcome; humans are humans so that they can overcome. So, it is futile to cry and agonize too much. "Overcome selfishness, ambition, everything which is evil in you! We have overcome before you, walk in our path." This is what the great teachers have always said, and this has encouraged human individuals. One after another has tried, struggled and fought, fallen and risen up. Every now and again a human has been born, who has reached so far that they have become a Bodhisattva, as it is called in India. This means that the person's true essence is bodhi, or wisdom, they have become a manifestation of wisdom, their essence is wisdom. Not many of these have been born from our humanity, but yet a few. Every Bodhisattva then has a chance to become a Buddha. In order to do that, the individual must be born many times as a Bodhisattva, which means that they must be born into the world many times for the purpose of working for the good of humanity and to teach humanity. The individual then teaches other people as a Bodhisattva when they themselves are akin to a personification of wisdom, when their essence is bodhi. Time after time the individual is born and teaches people in this way, and finally they are offered a chance to become a Buddha.

The old Indian systems describe to us that a certain Bodhisattva is, in a way, the highest Bodhisattva, holding the office of the teacher of humanity. Modern Theosophical writings state that the Bodhisattva is a being who teaches on Earth, but remains hidden from us. He can be born here, yet he also imparts teachings through his disciples. It is said that there are only a few of such Bodhisattvas in our history, in our evolution. The Bodhisattva who became the Buddha and appeared as the Buddha 500 years before Christ is now the previous Bodhisattva of humanity. When he became the Buddha, he handed over his crown to another being. In Indian literature, it is told that when the Bodhisattva of that time was born as Gautama in the Siddharta family, he took off his crown in heaven before he was born and placed it on the head of another Bodhisattva, who was destined to be the Bodhisattva of humanity after him. This Bodhisattva, who took the crown from the current Buddha 2500 years ago, still holds the highest office of teaching on Earth and enlightens humanity until he himself becomes a Buddha. Madame Blavatsky stated, in agreement with Indian books, that the current Bodhisattva will remain in this position for a few thousand years more before becoming a Buddha. It is said that he will become the Maitreya Buddha. When the Buddha said, "the Maitreya Buddha will come after me", some concluded that the Maitreya Buddha was Christ. However, Madame Blavatsky and other authors wrote that only after 5000 years from the Buddha will the current Bodhisattva become a Buddha, approximately 2500 years from now. This is an occult view, for even though some could think that Jesus Christ was the Maitreya Buddha, a more accurate and occultly correct perspective is not to refer to Jesus Christ as the Maitreya Buddha. Instead, we should consider Him as an entirely different being, as I will soon try to explain.

The current Bodhisattva, the present teacher, received his office from the previous Bodhisattva, the current Buddha. What does it mean that this previous Bodhisattva became the Buddha? It means that he was ready and had attained the highest possible human evolution: perfection. He will no longer be born on Earth as a human; he can be reborn within different people, but therein always lies a mystery. However, he himself will not be born as a human being. When one is a Bodhisattva, one holds the same position as the original professors of the original secret academy. When one becomes a Bodhisattva, whether holding an office or not, one is akin to a professor or a teacher. When one becomes a Buddha, one has given up the teacher's post, risen above it, become a living power, and completely merged into Christ, becoming a part of the Banyan tree. One can no longer be born on Earth as an ordinary human being, but one can enliven another human, inspire another highly evolved being on Earth, for one oneself is a living power. However, the one who became the Buddha in 500 B.C. could not, in his physical form, completely assimilate the Cosmic Christ, so it cannot be said of him that he planted on Earth the tree of life, the Banyan tree, the Cosmic Christ. He was not yet able to do so. His brains, reason, heart, and being had been fulfilled with the Cosmic Christ, but not conclusively. He himself only attained freedom in life, but not yet in death. There was still one secret left: the overcoming of death. The Buddha, of course, overcame death in his own life by constructing an invisible body in which he lives in the invisible world, but he did not overcome death in his physical body. He lived to an old age, but then he died, moving off into the spirit world. However, the overcoming of death was achieved by the first person to do so, Jesus Christ, who was born on Earth 500 years after the death of the Buddha. Jesus Christ was not the Bodhisattva to whom the Buddha left his teaching post, but He was a very peculiar being. We can say that the Buddha was reborn in Jesus, accompanying Him, as were many other wise ones of old times.

Jesus Christ was a being who, for hundreds of thousands of years, had listened to the voice of love, and had always lived according to the voice of His own heart, and had suffered everything done unto Him by humanity. He never believed in anything else but love; He never cared about anything else. He simply felt love and always followed that voice, even if it put Him against the whole world. He was so thoroughly pure in all His suffering and in overcoming Himself that He eventually was able to become what the Cosmic Christ had awaited for hundreds of thousands, even millions of years: when shall come the son of man into whom the Son of God could descend, when shall such a human being be born on Earth whom the Son of God could complete? Jesus Christ, who had grown in wisdom, humility, and beauty over the course of His lives, became this man into whom the Cosmic Christ could descend. This process transcended the divine academy, yet it was the purpose for which the academy existed. The academy had prepared for this process with the best of its abilities. Jesus had attended the school of Melchizedek over the course of many, many lives. He never harbored any evil nor committed any, and He was so purified that when He was born as Jesus of Nazareth, the heavenly academy recognized Him as the redeemer, the one who plants the Banyan tree among mankind. He brings the tree of life on Earth. Invisibly, all the high sages came to bow to Him when He was born.

Naturally, preparations had been made for the coming of Jesus Christ. However, one aspect of these preparations has disturbed and clouded the perception of some occultists. It is the notion that the Bodhisattva who followed the Buddha took on the task and mission to also prepare the ground for the coming of Jesus Christ, i.e., the tree of life. This Bodhisattva had a special influence on a being who lived a hundred years before Christ, a figure we have all read and heard about; Jesus ben Pandira or Yehoshua ben Pandira. The Talmud of the Jews and the Toldoth Jeshu tales from the Middle Ages talk about this being. It is a historical fact that a hundred years before Christ, there lived Jesus ben Pandira; a good, pure, and wise man. He taught the Jewish and Essene congregations, and according to the Talmud, he was captured, stoned to death, and hung on a tree. These events occurred around 100 B.C. Naturally, some occultists, looking back in time, have seen these events in nature's memory and concluded that this earlier Jesus is Jesus Christ, thus assuming that Jesus Christ must be the same as the Jesus of the Talmud. However, this is not true. Upon closer examinations these occultists have noticed that a hundred years after ben Pandira, an influential prophet lived in Judea. Yet, they have not been able to discern anything special about him.

Here is an important thing to note: attempting to see back in time through occult means to study the times of Jesus Christ on Earth in the Akasha without His permission would lead us astray. We must first become students of Jesus Christ, following His commandments. We must unite with the Cosmic Christ in our spirit and gain His permission to perceive things as they are; otherwise we can only see Jesus ben Pandira, who appears brighter and more radiant than the being, who lived in Judea a hundred years after him. If we are not with the spirit of Jesus Christ, we cannot see His aura, which covers the whole planet. His aura is as big as our Earth. If we, through occult means, reach Jesus Christ only partially, we will not be able to see His aura. We see the great auras: the auras of the Bodhisattvas and the Buddhas can appear magnificent and radiant, but the aura of Jesus Christ is so great that none of it can be seen without His permission. This has caused the misconception that Jesus Christ is the same as the current Bodhisattva, but this is inaccurate. The Bodhisattva is a separate being, a wonderful being, and while he may be referred to as Jesus due to his influence through Jesus ben Pandira and later Apollonius of Tyana, he is not Jesus Christ. Jesus Christ holds a unique position on our star; He is the life from which all Bodhisattvas derive their knowledge, the tree of life of which the Buddha is a branch, and of which all members of the White Brotherhood are branches.

Melchizedek still reigns, but Jesus Christ is the heir-apparent to the old king Melchizedek. Both continue to rule, but Jesus Christ is steadily gaining more power. Jesus Christ redeemed Earth's disguised being of light known as Satan or Lucifer, who is both the lightbringer of humanity and the devil. He is not evil himself: although his power entices men toward both good and evil, Jesus Christ has redeemed him. This is another mystery, but to put it briefly, it is no longer necessary for humans to suffer and experience everything; there's no longer a need to indulge in every pleasure and pain. This message, though two thousand years old, is still like new.

When discussing life and life experience in my youth, people wondered and asked me, "How will you truly understand life if you travel alone? You must engage with the world, participate in university life, be with friends, and experience everything; otherwise, you will not get to know anything." I wondered to myself: it is strange if we cannot become any wiser, if we must repeatedly experience the same things when we are born into this world, leaving us with little time to grow wiser. Why not as well say to me: you must steal a little, otherwise, you will not understand the life of a thief; you must murder or else you will not understand the emotional life of a murderer; you must make forgeries; you must get drunk to be able to understand the beauty within the soul of a drunkard. If we must always experience so much in this outer life, there will be no time for anything else. However, we do not need to do all that. Do the wise ones trust us enough that we do not need to undergo all those experiences? Of course. Humans have an instinctual knowledge of this if they do not believe in reincarnation. Yet, if one insists that we must engage in all worldly activities, be with friends, drink, and partake in various vices, we will not come to a conclusion. I thought to myself, that if one feels that one does not want to murder or steal, one could just as well say: "I do not want to waste time in any silliness, neither in societal life nor sitting around coffee tables. I want to study life, I want to understand it. I cannot study it in dance salons, around coffee tables, among friends. I can only study it within myself. If I cannot find God within myself, I cannot find Him without either."

As a matter of fact, human beings are called to think like this because the tree of life was planted within humankind. With the Cosmic Christ coming here through Jesus Christ, there is no longer any compulsion to sin; we can move forward in all that is good and overcome all evil.

We can become wise without having to have experienced all evil. We can consciously rise above all that we have experienced over the course of thousands of years. Eternal life awaits us everywhere and in every moment; this is Jesus Christ's gift to humanity. Eternal life is always awaiting us within ourselves, we need not seek it anywhere else.

II

THE PHASES OF THE LIFE OF SATAN

Many people might have wondered whether I believe in Satan when they saw today's lecture topic: "The Phases of the Life of Satan". If I state now that I do believe in Satan, it's important to keep in mind that I believe this matter has both a realistic side as well as a philosophical and metaphysical side. In the last lecture, we discussed Satan, and I attempted to describe him. However, there's yet another side to the matter: we must remember that the question of Satan is connected to the problem of evil in general. This question, too, has its own philosophical-metaphysical side.

The Christian dogma teaches that evil came into the world via the so-called Fall when people, unable to obey God's commandments, fell into sin. This raises a question within us: why did they fall into sin? This question was answered: people fell into sin because the devil, in the form of a snake, tempted them. While this explanation was practical, it gave rise to another question: who was the devil that led the first people into sin? The answer came: the devil was a fallen angel, the leader of great angelic forces, akin to all the other leaders of angelic forces, perhaps even more beautiful, handsome, and gorgeous. Guided by their chief angel, these angelic troops looked at themselves and realized how beautiful they were. The sin of pride came upon them. When they compared themselves to others and saw that they were as beautiful as God, they fell into their own vanity and rebelled against God. Thus, these angels fell into sin.

That fallen angel might have actually existed, but this story does not explain the philosophical side of the matter; it only pushes the core of the problem even further. We ask: from where did this pride come to the angels, and why did they fall? If God had created the angels, just like He had created everyone else, then what was wrong with these angels? From where could evil have come into those few? These metaphysical questions remained unanswered for they were incomprehensible; the question of evil could not be solved. Its mysteries were unsolvable for it was one of God's secrets. However, as we learned to think on our own, it did not occur to us that this question would be forbidden and it should not be reflected upon. We understand that humans have reason, and this reason must seek an answer, turning the whole question philosophical. We no longer cared to ask about Satan or his troops of war, but we simply asked: how did evil come into the world? We received an answer: there have been two forces from the beginning, good and evil, God and the devil, constantly in conflict, just like in the teachings of Zoroaster – whose understanding of this doctrine is not quite right – in the doctrine called dualism. Dualism posits that there are two forces, good and evil, which are in eternal conflict with each other. However, we find it obvious that there is only one God, one secret of existence, the origin of both evil and good. Therefore, God must be behind evil as well. That is as far as we can reach with our reasoning. It is comforting to know that the perennial wisdom Madame Blavatsky proclaimed to the world has always emphasized that there is only one principle of life, one foundation of existence, whether it is called God or the absolute or whatever. This principle is God, the farthest and most unattainable principle we can understand. This one divine life is behind both good and evil, light and darkness. It is above all opposites. It is the bottomless abyss engulfing everything. It is the unmanifested from which everything manifests. It is the absolute encompassing all opposites. Therefore, this absolute is responsible for the potential of evil as well as the potential of good.

What is evil? When we attempt to solve this problem philosophically, through perennial, esoteric, and internal wisdom, we arrive at the same conclusion Madame Blavatsky referred to in the Secret Doctrine: the origin of evil lies in humans. Although Divinity, i.e., the absolute life, contains the potential of evil, its manifested origin is always in humans. What is a human? As we explained last time, a human is a manifestation of conscious life in a limited form. In other words, a human is life, or consciousness, limited as the self. That self, that idea of the self, originates and discloses evil. The potential for selfhood to arise exists within the absolute. Without the ability for selfhood to be born, no manifestation could exist or serve any purpose. However, when the self is born, so is evil. All manifestation is based on limitation, and that is the metaphysical origin of evil. The unmanifested life is inherently limitless. There can be no manifestation in limitlessness or infinity. Infinity is the same as emptiness and non-manifestation; it is the infinite eternity in which there is nothing. It is the absolute, but within it lies the potential for manifestation, for limitation. The entirety of manifested life is limitation. Limitation inevitably leads to selfhood, and with it comes the potential for evil.

The absolute life has two sides we call consciousness and form or spirit and matter. These two sides are joined in the manifestation. The unmanifested is limited into form, in which lives the consciousness. This limited consciousness will inevitably lead to selfhood. The consciousness would in no way be aware of its own form without a selfhood being born in it. If we think of stones, which are a limited manifestation of life, we are unable to perceive the selfhood in them. It is an entirely different fact altogether that there exists a consciousness, an imperceptible selfhood, behind the mineral kingdom. Therefore, we say that while a stone represents a form of limitation, it has not yet attained consciousness, or selfhood, for it cannot observe itself. The same applies to plants. We can find selfhood in the vegetable kingdom if we enter the consciousness of a plant, but we cannot perceive it in all the plants we see. We do not really see selfhood in animals either, although we notice that consciousness is more manifest in them than it is in plants or stones. We observe that an animal feels and thinks, but it hardly thinks like a human self-being, because it is completely ruled by its instincts. Therefore, we must find the selfhood of an animal somewhere else. Human beings are forms containing selfhoods. In every human, there is a discerning, thinking, and aspiring selfhood, who knows itself and can compare itself to others and to the surrounding world and judge itself. When we look around us, we surely cannot state that stones are evil because they do not think about themselves. We cannot say so about plants either. We would rather say that plants are kind and good. Likewise, we say that animals are rather good. Even when they are savage beasts, they are not evil in the ethical sense, for they act based on their instincts. Consciousness can be best observed in domestic animals. For example, we can see the first indications of selfhood in dogs, but we cannot call it an ethical selfhood; this we observe only in human beings, who are responsible for their words and actions. Nobody can do whatever they like without the society coming after them and saying that they have committed evil and broken the laws. The human self is the creator of evil. That, which I know to be an ethically responsible being, brings forth evil. One can be either good or evil: one can follow the law or break it. A human being brings evil into the world, and thus it is imperative that we understand what we mean by a human being. We do not refer to a creature that merely outwardly appears human or looks like us; instead, we refer to a responsible being capable of reasoning, judging, and thinking, one that carries the burden of life as a responsible being. This selfhood is the one bringing forth evil. The potential for evil exists in God because in Him, there is the potential for limitation, but evil comes into the manifested world through a self-being. This is the philosophical side of the matter.

We must remember, as we discussed last time, that this life and existence in which we all partake is neither random nor a pointless game of the forces of nature; rather, it is a cosmos arranged according to a great principle. It is a school for all centers of consciousness. What kind of school is it? Does it have a purpose? Does existence itself have a purpose? These philosophical questions are often presented. I have been asked many times about the purpose of life and the purpose of the great absolute God. To this question, which is a double-edged sword, we respond: the absolute God and life itself does not have a purpose. What purpose could God, the absolute life, have? Existence has no purpose other than itself; the purpose of existence is to exist. It is a necessity, and necessity cannot have any purpose. Our reason requires the purpose to be known, even if it cannot be defined. What purpose is this? It is the inner bliss of existence. It is the practical solution to the problem, for if we think practically, we instantly feel within ourselves and deep within our consciousness that if something is harmonious, pure, beautiful, and true, then it must be inherently good. Therefore, the great purpose is absolute bliss and happiness, and there does not need to be any other purpose. Some philosophers have said that the purpose of existence is eternal bliss and happiness. However, that is not a philosophical answer derived from reason, but rather an answer stemming from emotion. The philosophical answer is that there is no theological explanation for the purpose of existence. All theological explanations for it are meaningless. Existence is because it is.

However, that explanation only pertains to the great divinity itself. When it comes to manifestations and limitations, we ask: what purpose do they have? Then we receive the answer: every form has a purpose, whether it be a flower, an animal, a human being, an angel, or a manifested center of consciousness. What are these purposes? We say: the purpose of the mineral kingdom is to be free, and it attains its freedom in the vegetable kingdom. The mineral kingdom is bound to rigid forms and therefore cannot think beyond perhaps some material thoughts. The vegetable kingdom is much freer. The vegetable kingdom yearns and strives to become the animal kingdom. The animal kingdom yearns and strives to become mankind. Mankind strives and aspires, writhes in agony, lives through hells and heavens to become the kingdom of angels. Therefore, we can say; the purpose of a human being is to become an angel. Practically speaking, the purpose of a human is to resolve the conflict between good and evil. The purpose of a human is to be free of the lower self and evil, and to become totally good, become an angel and God. We can call these things by different names, but they are all just the next step in the great evolution. Only after a human being has relinquished evil, conquered it within themselves, and reached the angelic state will something new be revealed to them, allowing them to see new possibilities before them. Absolutely unforeseen, wonderful, and enchanting possibilities in total bliss and happiness open up for them. Life does not end when one overcomes evil: life begins when one overcomes evil.

A human being has a definite purpose. Modern Theosophy teaches that a human being is destined to become a Master. I agree: the purpose of a human being is to become a Master. A Master is a being who has overcome evil within themselves, overcome all selfishness, and become an angel. Theosophical literature often notes that a Master is above angels. Therefore, we must remember that when a person has become a Master, they are above many kinds of spiritual beings, or angels. By the term angel, I refer to those groups of angels in Earth's atmosphere and in our Solar System. A person who, in their evolution, reaches the state of Master belongs to the eminent group above those groups of angels. There is a notable difference between a name and a fact. Madame Blavatsky did not state in the Secret Doctrine that humanity will become a group of angels, but rather a group of gods, and it is better to phrase it like this to avoid misunderstandings. When we ask how people become angels, gods, and Master-beings, we must remember from our last discussion that all Theosophical literature teaches that this evolution does not happen by itself or by nature. Theosophical literature does not say that humanity was left to develop on its own, but instead, it says that this development is happening according to a precisely organized system. Just as we have an organized society with its schools and universities in this visible life, we understand that the great world has been organized as a school for us. We have both teachers and also those who attempt to lead us off the right path.

This brings us to Satan. We remember that Satan, who can technically be called the ruler of the world, is an unbelievably grand angel, a high divine being, and one of the highest rulers of our solar system. As you recall, the Book of Jacob mentioned that Satan is one of the great angels participating in God's negotiation. Satan represents Earth, and the other participants in this joint negotiation are the divine angelic beings of our Solar System. Satan is probably one of the most beautiful and luminous angels in this council board of gods because he has taken on the mission to keep a school for human beings who must resolve the problem of good and evil. This entails a tremendously great renouncement. He cannot show himself at all; he must only give his great power to the use of human beings and cover himself up, disguise himself. Only poetry portrays him differently; the truth is that as a divine being, he has undertaken an unspeakable renouncement. What is this renouncement? It is that he cannot directly use his own goodness and wisdom. Instead, he must let others manifest both his goodness and his wisdom, and he must give his powers to the use of others. We cannot, at the moment, find a metaphor for this in our everyday life because nothing in our everyday life can truly describe such great ethical sanctity. We are way too small to find suitable metaphors for this great renouncement. However, as moral human beings, we can appreciate the greatness of the renouncement demanded of Satan. Driven by command and love for the beings who must now evolve, he has to renounce everything and give his creative power to the misuse of rather ignorant beings. As we pointed out the last time, the goodness and wisdom possessed by our planet's luminous original leader, Earth's planetary spirit Satan, were given on behalf of him for others to rule and guide. We remember how a group of highly evolved beings came here from other stars and established the secret academy; the central school of eternal wisdom, the Secret Brotherhood. These ones who came from elsewhere had access to all of Satan's wisdom and knowledge, and they were allowed to use it. They organized an evolutionary school for people here on our Earth and oversaw the evolution of mankind; they held the position of teacher, and thus represented the good, bright, right, and beautiful side of the task of Satan.

We humans are divine beings, for the human being was born when God's love focused on the soul of an animal giving birth to selfhood. We are beings born of divinity belonging to the group of good beings; we are a group of angels, although not yet a very evolved group of angels. We have received this Earth as our evolutionary school, and as good beings, we represent the good in the planetary spirit of Earth, Satan. Therefore, as good beings ourselves, we are, in a way, part of this secret brotherhood. When the brotherhood comes here, our highest self will not resist it, but will be on their side, even though we are subject to their teachings.

We must remember that there is another side to this subject. While the highest part of us, our actual self, belongs to this good group representing the wisdom, goodness, truth, light, and knowledge of Satan, we humans also, at the same time, belong to another group as well, based on the fact that we are human selfhoods and evil can arise in us. We humans go to a school of contradictions. We are of two kind; we are both in the group of the good and noble in our highest self, and also in the fallen black group, the selfish group, attending this aforementioned school in order to develop as human beings; to learn about good and evil. Because it is unlikely that we were left alone in this black selfhood and darkness, we cannot be called self-aware devils. Only as human children do we possess the potential and the necessity to create evil. We create evil, but it is at first very weak and unaware. Even in this evil, we are taught by a great and manifold group who came here from elsewhere, spiritual beings whose special task is to draw out all the evil that is in us, so that we learn to choose between good and evil. Just as the great adepts, who came here from elsewhere, represent all the good beings here, these evil beings likewise have their representatives who have come from elsewhere. Evil beings who, in their evolution, are at the stage where they have not yet overcome evil in themselves, but are more evolved in their own conflict than many other infant humans. However, there are some who, at least momentarily, have perhaps chosen evil and selfishness, chosen to oppose God, and chosen all darkness and all possible power to oppose the laws of evolution.

Our planet is a peculiar school, a wondrous stage for a unique drama. Here, we encounter high initiates, remarkably high angelic beings, deities, and Master-beings, alongside all kinds of evil beings descending deeper into materialism and selfishness, attempting to draw others with them. We live our lives surrounded by demons. Of course, if we become materialists, freedom might seem appealing to us: when there is no concept of good or evil, one can do as they please. However, this is a mistaken view: one fails to recognize that they are surrounded by a large group of so-called white beings, ready to help them in all goodness and to advise them and teach them, as well as a large group of black beings, waiting to grab them when they are weak. This is not something to fear, but rather a tremendous show of life's confidence in us; a testament to life's trust in human selves, trusting that they can navigate both hell and heaven. Human selves must overcome all challenges and become so powerful in everything good that they can interact with divine beings as equals. Why do we cower in fear when faced with divine beings, and flee at the sight of devils and other black beings? What sort of humans are we then? No! We must become true humans and men so that we fear no evil. A man is someone who has overcome fear, standing firm like a rock when storms try to plunge him down, knowing that, as an eternal human, he stands unwavering even if the world falls apart around him. We humans must cultivate this masculine aspect within ourselves to become individuals who remain calm, neither defending themselves nor fussing about, nor resorting to violence by grabbing swords or pistols, nor by attacking another, but instead standing serene and peaceful when beasts maul them or their brothers crucify them. Therein lies the true masculinity of the human being.

And what of the femininity of the human being? Just as essential as masculinity, the femininity of the human being emerges when an individual is surrounded by everything good, when light envelops them, and all earthly happiness and beauty flows towards them. The individual stands calmly and peacefully, rejoicing in their purity. Such an individual can receive all this happiness, peace, bliss, and light without cynicism, pessimism, bitterness, or doubt, rejoicing because their own heart is completely pure. The femininity of the human being lies in being able to respond to this great light and love with equal measures of light and love.

Therefore, we can say that humans participate in a peculiar and wisely organized school. Our task is now to start exploring those so-called Falls and the evil tempters – Lucifer, Beelzebub, Ahriman, Satan, and others – who harass us and make us lapse. We must also study the heavenly wars, in which the forces of good fight against the forces of evil. The wars waged to help our lives and evolution here on Earth.

III

DO DEMONS EXIST?

Throughout human history, there has always existed a belief in spirits, both good and evil. In ancient Persia, they believed in the crown prince of evil spirits, Ahriman. However, they did not believe in the eternity of evil or the eternal power of Ahriman. They believed that the good Ormuzd would win in the end, that light would finally overcome darkness. Only Christianity – we should add medieval Christianity – invented the eternal crown prince of evil and the concept of eternal damnation. This dubious credit indeed befalls upon the Christendom.

As seekers of truth, as Theosophists and Rosicrucians, when we study and discuss evil, evil spirits, and for instance Satan, I feel as my moral responsibility to remind us of the fact that true evil does not exist. There is no eternal god of evil or eternal damnation. It is vital for us to remember this. We acknowledge the existence of evil spirits, even ones we can outright refer to as Satans, but there is no personified crown prince of evil, and there is no eternal damnation. This notion of eternal damnation has tormented humanity for centuries, but this nightmare is now starting to fade into its own black non-existence. Despite this, we know that the

Christendom still officially believes in the existence of evil and eternal damnation, although the practical prevalence of this belief is diminishing. Even here in Finland, these days, there are not many people who would want to emphasize and teach the doctrine of eternal damnation. However, those concerned might not yet officially dare to deny it. Therefore, it is necessary for the enlightened group seeking truth and acknowledging the existence of spirit to proclaim loud and clear that evil as an eternal reality does not exist, and neither does eternal damnation or hell.

I would like to remind us of a few, perhaps familiar, tales that speak of this eternity of evil, i.e., damnation. These tales are good to remember, and they can help those who are still under the spell of disbelief.

An old tale recounts that damned souls, in their distress and agony, once turned to the God of the world and prayed, "O', place on our necks a millstone as great as the greatest mountain – no matter how big it is and no matter how much it weighs on us – but let a small bird, a small nightingale, fly to us once every hundred years and rub its beak on this millstone. If this little nightingale comes every hundred years to rub its beak on it, then we have hope that someday the millstone will wear out. Then, we have hope that one day, after endless eons, we will be free from this pain."

Another old tale coming from the East – for all nations have believed in hell – tells the following: "God, the Lord and Creator of worlds, sat on his throne in the middle of the wonderful Heaven, surrounded by countless groups of angels. All these radiant beings, living in bliss with the Lord, slowly danced and sang praises, 'Glory be, glory be to the Lord in Heaven.' Their communal song resounded unspeakably beautiful. However, when they finished their song, some sort of reverberation sounded throughout space – a strangely sad, but touching sound, the sound of singing. The Lord God listened from his throne, and after a while, he asked: 'Where is this touchingly beautiful sound coming from?' One of the chief angels rose before the Lord and said, 'O' thou Lord and Creator of Earth and Heaven, it is the singing of the voices of the millions of souls in hell.' 'Is that so?' said God, contemplating for a moment. Then, raising his head, he said, 'Because their singing is so beautiful, they must be set free.' Immediately, God instructed that all 49 keys to hell be given to an angel, who, accompanied with his aides, went into hell to open all the gates. Out came all the souls, singing a praise so wonderful and beautiful that never had been heard any song more beautiful, more wonderful. The Lord God wanted to listen to this song over and over again."

Then there is a third little anecdote that comes to mind. It is not an allegorical myth; rather, it might be a real historical event. It is told that when Catholics began to spread Christianity to the Scandinavian countries – St. Ansgar had decided that Christianity needed to be spread to Scandinavia – noble and eloquent speeches were held in various places in Sweden. The missionaries depicted all the misery, agony, torment, and damnation awaiting those unfortunate ones who did not want to embrace Christianity. The missionaries also beautifully and vividly depicted the joy of those who were baptized, portraying all that they would inherit in eternity. Their speeches were effective: they stirred the crowds, and even the old Vikings were baptized. Among them was an old Viking prince, who appeared thoughtful, noble, and elegant. Lost in thought he also stepped forth to be baptized. Just as the priest was about to baptize him, the noble prince asked, "What about those who have lived before us and were not baptized? Where are all my ancestors, all my relatives, all my friends; where are they?" "They are, of course, in eternal damnation and hell," replied the missionary. "Is that so?" said this old Viking, "In that case, I do not wish to be baptized, for my place is where my friends, my relatives, and my ancestors are. I cannot be happy elsewhere; I want to go to damnation and hell with them."

These little stories and other such legends and anecdotes are good to remember when we try to counter the belief in eternal damnation. In our eyes, such belief seems impossible. We are not haunted by such thoughts, and it is unlikely that anyone would want to delve into them even for a moment. Such contemplation would undoubtedly result in the loss of one's sanity or faith. Even though we do not believe in any kind of eternal damnation or any eternal prince of darkness, any personified supreme crown prince of evil, we still understand that behind all such notions lies some esoteric truth. When Christian monks invented this eternal Satan and eternal damnation – and thus eternal evil – they may have realized the truth that the potential of evil is eternal. Evil is always connected to humanity; there is no evil in the universe without a human being giving birth to it, no evil without a human being, who is able to discern the opposites and discriminate between them. Only humans give rise to evil, as it would be ethically unjust to deem evil the fact that existence is suffering. Suffering is something derived from life itself, from existence itself. Those who are morally evolving and growing within do not see existence as suffering, but rather as a blessing. They may say that suffering is a great school; suffering is only a natural consequence of the laws of nature being broken. It is surely nature's goodness that is revealed in suffering, not nature's evil.

Evil will, in its ethical significance, can only exist in a human, a self-being, who has the wonderful freedom, this downright inevitable freedom, to be mean, malicious, selfish, and cruel. Humans have been given this freedom so they can learn to choose good, for no being is truly ethical if its goodness is merely a natural trait. An individual who is good-natured, who is too lazy to be mean, is still not a good being. An individual is good only when they have overcome evil, when they have consciously renounced all evil and embraced good. We cannot even imagine a divine being, a high being who would not be ethically perfect, whose will would not be so perfect and pure that we could trust them completely. What is a being who has not experienced anything? Of course, a child is innocently beautiful and lovely, but we have no guarantee that if a child is presented with a temptation, it can resist succumbing to it. A child is lovely and beautiful in its innocence, but when the strange temptations and allurements of life come, the child may fall. Of course, some children can resist the fall, but most cannot. Such an individual, still metaphorically akin to a child, no matter how beautiful or seemingly good, is not eternally good and trustworthy until they have passed through fire, until they have been purified in the fire of agonies, and have learned to stand firm in the midst of all temptations. What is a being who still falls into sin, iniquity, and evil? It is not yet a trustworthy being. It is still a common human being attending the school of suffering, not a divine being. A divine being, an ethically trustworthy being, is one who, in all eternities, is in the service of good. A divine being is a master over evil, capable of making evil serve them. Only such a being is truly trustworthy in their goodness, for they have gone through the school. Therefore, from an ethical point of view, we cannot say any evil can exist, except for the potential evil within a human being, within the human self, which the individual must overcome.

This school of life, this school of good and evil, is immensely long. It is not finished in one day or one lifetime. When we look at the human souls attending this school, we see that some of them are good and others evil; some can be more good than evil and some more evil than good. There are naturally many beings in this universe of ours who are extremely evil, in whom evil is in the foreground, but all beings are essentially good. All are essentially divine. Goodness is like a seed planted in the heart of every being, but this goodness cannot flourish until the being has attended the school of good and evil, has learned to discern the opposites, and learned to choose good. Therefore, there are many beings in whom evil appears predominant. Even among human beings, there are souls who are cruel, mean, and vicious, who appear to enjoy doing harm and evil. We have vindictiveness within us. We get mad and angry, we want to use violence, we want to oppress, and we want justice to prevail at any cost. All kinds of cruelty still lie in us human beings. We are not yet definitively good beings.

When we look at these things from the spiritual viewpoint and not from the viewpoint of this visible life, we observe that there is a tremendous number of demons on this planet. Human beings themselves make for excellent demons. Among humans, there are great numbers of all kinds of evil spirits. In other words, when one looks at human souls, one sees all kinds of animals. The animal in us is always prone to doing evil. In this visible world, we may look like angels, but in the soul world we appear as all kinds of beasts: wolves, pigs, bulls, tigers, snakes, dragons, and such. It is as if people are still "possessed by evil spirits," to use the New Testament phrasing. The animals within us are not a part of ourselves. We as humans are rational beings who yearn for the perfection of God, who yearn for light, goodness, truth, and beauty. We do not yearn for anything base, anything animalistic, vicious, or cruel. We yearn for all things beautiful, but our yearning is very deep within, and we remember it only now and then. Thus, we think that this animal in us is of our true self.

It is important to note that in this Solar System, or even on this planet, there are not only human beings, but also countless groups of beings who are not human, are not clad in human form, although they may be at a similar stage of evolution to human beings. They may be at the stage where they must pass through the human crisis. However, they do not inhabit the physical world like human beings; instead, they live in the soul world. The countless numbers of such beings establish that the belief in the existence of evil spirits across diverse cultures is not a delusion. It has simply been forgotten that the evil spirits reside within ourselves, and those spirits outside cannot harm us unless we have similar evil beings within. The evil spirits in the invisible world pose no threat to us, for nature has given us our physical body for protection. We are, as long as we live in this physical body, under the protection of God, under the protection of all good forces of nature. The evil ones cannot harm us. Only when we open our hearts to them, when we harbor demons within ourselves, can we be infiltrated by evil beings.

We notice that among all peoples, there have always been varied attempts to appease these evil beings of nature. They have been offered sacrifices, blood has been shed, and all sorts of things have been done to gain their favor towards human beings. However, it would have been wiser to outright drive these demons out of human beings, instead of trying to gain their favor. That would have been the best measure against evil. The different cultures of the world have not yet understood that there are evil spirits within humans themselves. One nation which today is immersed in the belief in spirits and evil demons is, as we know, the people of Tibet. Everyone over there has amulets, prayer wheels, and all kinds of items with which they protect themselves against evil spirits. They always have all kinds of ceremonies, processions, and the like to protect themselves. However, the Tibetans rarely think that one should purify oneself and thus be free from the power of all evil spirits. Of course, there are some individuals who think so, but in general most people do not believe that. We here in Europe are not as much under the influence of these beliefs, and that is why I mentioned Tibet, which is, as we say, "under superstition." It is not really superstition, but simply an unenlightened and unwise belief.

Now that we understand how evil as a manifested reality originates in human beings, we can move on to the history of evil. It is customary to differentiate three distinct eras in the history of humanity. First is the era which the old traditions and tales call the golden era – aetas aurea. It was a time when humanity lived in paradise, in perfect harmony, not yet knowing evil. The second era is the time when evil manifests, confronting humanity and ensnaring it under its spell. In the third era humanity no longer knows evil, for it has overcome evil, and good alone lives among humanity. This is the third era.

Today, we are still living in this second phase, or era. The third phase is the vision of the future all prophets foretell. The time has always been prophesied when all people live in mutual harmony, when all animals, both wild beasts and domestic animals, and small children share a meadow together: a tiger licks a child's feet; a small girl hangs on a lion's neck; and a wolf sleeps next to a lamb. This time has always been prophesied. All the people have then beaten their swords into plowshares and live in brotherhood together. This is the future vision of a millennial kingdom which has not yet come. We do not yet live in this third phase, but neither do we live in the first phase anymore. We live in the period in which evil fights against good. We live in the phase where the opposites appear so very clear.

We can also clearly differentiate three smaller phases in this middle era we now live in. When we inspect the history of the evolution of humanity, three different phases become evident. The first phase in this second great era is the beginning of evil. Indeed, evil once had a historical beginning, symbolically referred to as the Fall. It is discussed in old Chaldean tales. Then there is the second phase, where evil rises to its peak. In the third phase, good begins its fight against evil, leading to a constant battle between the two forces.

In which phase do we live? Of course, we now live in this third phase. We have already been released from the ensnares of those first two phases, the fall to evil and the rise of evil to its peak. Now prevails this battle between good and evil. However, this battle is by no means eternal, for it will inevitably end in the victory of good.

If we now wish to take a glance at the evolutionary history of evil, or the phases of our mankind – I mean a general overview, for we cannot delve into details now, otherwise, it would take too long – we must remember the following requisite, which is familiar from all Theosophical readings and studies and which I have always tried to emphasize: we as human beings have received this human body as a gift from nature. In other words, our home as human spiritual beings is in a different world, in the inner spiritual world. We are from this inner world, and we have received the human body so that we can attend school, so that we can learn and develop. As human spiritual beings, as self-beings, we are something other than this body. This body is more perfect than what we are. The physicians and anatomists who have studied the human body and its functions universally acknowledge it as a remarkably wisely created organism. Neither we nor them would state that this body is our own creation. At least we have no recollection of it. When we are born here on Earth, we all receive the human body as a gift from our parents. The body is very undeveloped at first, but as the child develops, the body develops and becomes a better instrument for the human being.

The body originally belonged to another line of evolution, the physical line of evolution. We ourselves are spiritual beings belonging to a different evolutionary line. This is clearly seen from the way we humans, who now live here as mankind, lived as the animal kind on another star before we were born here. In other words, we lived as the animal kind during our Earth's earlier incarnation, which we are accustomed to call the Moon-Manvantara. We do not describe those animals here; we only say that we lived as an animal kind similar to our current animal kingdom. Maybe it was not as perfect as the current one, but that earlier animal kind had all the natural principles of animals; the animals could move, give birth, and lust, just like the current animals. While living as this animal kind, we, at least the most of us, were born as humans, as the human self, into this animal body. This happened when the immortal spirit behind everything descended into this animal, giving birth to the human self. This is understandably an occult event. So, we were born as human selves in the Moon-Manvantara. However, that meant that those animal bodies were no longer suitable for us, as the human self needed a new kind of a body in order to exist and live. A totally different kind of organism was required for the human being, who must evolve in the knowledge of good and evil. Therefore, as human selves, we had to wait in Heaven until we could assume the human form. We had to wait for the physical evolution of Earth to progress. The physical bodies had to evolve from the protoplasm until it was possible to create the human body. We as human beings were not able to assist in this process; instead totally different kinds of beings were providing aid and support for this natural evolution. It was not superficial help but rather the kind of help that is selfless and self-sacrificing. As it is said in the Secret Doctrine, the Lunar Pitris and Solar Pitris, those high human beings who had completed the human stage of evolution, were assisting in the gradual formation of the human body on Earth. Meanwhile, we slept in the heavens, having beautiful dreams. We could not participate in the creation of our physical forms. Therefore, the human body is a gift from both nature and the higher beings. However, evolution is always also advancement, so we must not think that the human bodies, which were gradually being created, were perfect in their beauty and loveliness; far from it. When our scientific researchers study early humans from millions of years ago, they notice that these early humans looked exactly like apes back then. The human form has gradually taken its present appearance. Still, since the beginning, there has been a specific image – the human image – that the process of creation has tried to follow. What has been created has been inherently human from the beginning.

Let us imagine that, on one side, our human bodies are being created here on our planet. Our spirits, our stars, lie behind these human bodies, awaiting the moment when selfhoods can finally incarnate into them. When we look at this situation, we see that the human bodies have already assumed a form, but the form does not yet resemble present human beings; instead, the bodies are gigantic, huge – and hermaphroditic. So, we see that these bodies are about to be finished. On the other side, we see those human selves waiting in the heavens. Some of these selfhoods are a little older than others, meaning they were born slightly earlier as humans in the previous Moon-Manvantara. There are human souls, human selfhoods, of different ages.

Then a voice echoes through space: "Human selves, incarnate into those mindless forms specifically prepared for you." When we now look at these human souls in the heavens, we can see that two-thirds of them immediately follow the order and incarnate into those physical bodies. They have no second thoughts about it. All those younger souls in the heavens, who were born later as humans, obey the order and incarnate immediately. They do not think for themselves; they are still incredibly unevolved infant souls. Their minds have no reach. However, there is another group in the heavens – comprising one-third of the souls – who had been humans a bit longer than the rest, and consequently, had more experience. When they receive the order to incarnate, they glance at those physical vehicles prepared for them on Earth, and say, "No, we will not incarnate into them." The old religious myths call this the Fall of Angels. It is also referred to in the Book of Revelations. One-third of the souls said: "We will not incarnate, at least not yet." What was the reason for this thought? Was it malign will, stubbornness against God? No, we must understand this matter correctly. These human souls are thinking, "These bodies are yet not evolved enough for us; they are not yet the way we need them to be. It would be useless for us to be born into them for it would take infinite eons until we could evolve back to our current stage. We will only incarnate into those bodies when they become more evolved. We want to help nature. We want to help humanity."

We can understand their reasoning with a metaphor from everyday life. Let us imagine there is a father and a mother and they have a lot of children. These children have to go to school, but there is only one school in their area and it begins at the first grade. Here in our society, we have all kinds of schools and classes, so we can, of course, put our children into whatever grade we want, but let us focus on this specific example for now. The parents have already homeschooled some of their older children. Therefore, they can put their younger children in the first grade, but it would be useless to put those more evolved children in that grade. It would be an absolutely useless experience for the older children to attend the first grade if they have already studied everything beforehand. The same applies to humanity as a whole. The Fall of Angels was not the moral downfall it has been portrayed as. It was something totally natural and sensible from the human point of view.

However, from all this followed a tragedy in the history of our humanity, which perhaps gave reason for people to depict the Fall of Angels as a lamentable incident. The youngest of all humans were unevolved souls, very child-like beings, who lived in absolute paradise during the first era of the paradise. However, their life in constant ignorance and happiness would not have led anywhere; it would have not led to any development. Therefore, they had to learn something. This presented an opportunity to the peculiar human beings of the Moon-Manvantara, who had not yet reached the level of development required of them in the Moon-Manvantara. Thus, they needed more education and experience; they had to repeat a grade, so to speak. However, the experience they needed was more of the psychological kind. They did not have to directly incarnate into human forms; instead, they could gain experience by possessing us regular humans. All traditions refer to these beings as evil spirits, often as Lucifer-beings. These beings descended to Earth taking over its mindless humanity and began to possess it. They entered our souls, so that we, who were rather mindless and thoughtless, felt some kind of a spiritual power within us. It was as if a voice had spoken inside of us, saying, "There is no time to be lazy. You are a human being; you must learn to think and you must accomplish something. You cannot just exist and live. You must learn to know good and evil." Of course, they did not phrase it like this, as humanity could not yet use language the way we do now. We received the message as images, as visions, and it startled our souls. We thought, "We really must learn something; we must know something. We are somehow different from those other beings we see around us." The Lucifer-beings tempted us: "Look at those animals around you; they breed and multiply. You must copulate like animals." Humans had been totally innocent before; they had not known anything about sex, for they had been hermaphrodites. However, humans now started imitating animals, and this truly was like a fall to sin. We let the creative power within ourselves become the sexual power. At the same time, this was inevitable; it was our prerequisite for entering the school of life. Humanity fell into sin by choosing the pleasures of sexual intercourse over natural reproduction. This marked the beginning of the school of life, for these were the first opposites humanity learned to discern. Human beings learned to enjoy themselves, they learned to seek pleasures; and this was then followed by the counter-effect; suffering. This was the first Fall.

When humanity had fallen into sin, we, the rest of the human-gods who were in the heavens, decided to incarnate. We thought that we could help humanity: "Now we will incarnate into those tainted beings." However, instead of us having been able to redeem them, we also fell. This was because, at the same time as us, other not yet fully evolved beings from an even earlier era, the Sun era, incarnated. These beings are usually called the Ahrimans. They were born here as humans, but they were beings who sought power over nature and the knowledge of all the powers of nature. They were rather powerful and beautiful people among us, seeking the secrets of nature and, in a way, serving as an example to us. They got us excited about this visible life. That which to us in the heavens had felt so very imperfect and repulsive now began to attract us. The example of those Sun-people lead us to sin, to experiences of sexuality and sexual pleasure. Thus, all humanity had fallen into materialism. This was an inevitable experience, and therefore it was good: on one hand, it was a fall into evil, but on the other hand it was good. We had to learn to discern the opposites.

When humanity was at this stage of its evolution, a voice from the direction of the Sun echoed yet again through space: "Humanity will not fare on its own on this planet; teachers are needed from elsewhere to help it." The Secret Brotherhood came here and founded the central academy and taught our young humanity to do the work required of us after we had fallen into the cycle of rebirth. We had to maintain our bodies here on Earth. The conditions on Earth evolved gradually during millions of years and millennia into what they are now. Those wise ones who had come from elsewhere taught us how to plow the field; they brought us crops; they taught us to speak. They taught us everything. This was the first phase, the beginning of evil. After that comes the second phase, when evil reaches its peak.

IV

THE ETERNAL FIGHT

When we examine the problem of evil and its evolution throughout human history, we can differentiate three phases in the manifestation and evolution of evil. The first phase is the birth of evil, the second is the rise of evil to its peak, and the third is the battle of good against evil. Together, these three phases constitute the second of those great eras we have delineated in the history of humanity, based on the manifestation of good and evil.

In our previous lecture we explored the birth of evil, noting that it occurred millions of years ago on the continents known as Lemuria and Atlantis. It was in Lemuria wherein the birth of evil primarily took place, a birth referred to in religious books as the Fall to sin. The birth of evil was connected to the awakening of sexual power in human beings. Humans used to be hermaphroditic, having been sexless before that. Eventually humans were divided into two sexes during a long phase of evolution in human history. I would like to briefly mention two things here. First, we Christians usually follow the Old Testament in asserting that woman was created from the rib of man, a belief that has, as we know, caused a lot of ridicule. Adam fell into a deep sleep, during which a rib was taken from him, and God fashioned a wife for Adam from it.

From a linguistic point of view, it's noteworthy that the deity depicted as the creator in this story is referred to by a rather peculiar name: Elohim. This word "Elohim" is plural, indicating multiple gods rather than a singular god. What is even more peculiar is that this plural word carries a masculine suffix, despite its singular form being feminine. I think this suggests that those who wrote down this story wanted to express that these creative powers, or gods, were not exclusively masculine any more than they were feminine, but rather hermaphroditic. These creative powers, these gods, were thus goddess-gods, or hermaphrodite gods. It is important not to confuse this hermaphroditism with the physiological meaning of the word "hermaphroditism" here on Earth. The hermaphroditic nature of the name Elohim indicates that these creative powers represent both the male and the female principles. Psychologically they represent the masculine and feminine qualities, and metaphysically, or one might even dare to say physiologically, they represent both powers.

Let us consider an example: Every artist, writer, poet, inventor, or even a war chief, who is a true genius, understands that they must be influenced by two powers within themselves to create. One of these powers is inspiration, as every true genius is characterized by this power of inspiration. It is akin to a flash of light from above, from the higher worlds, that illuminates the soul of the genius. In that flash the genius is able to see and hear limitless amounts of things. Mozart claimed that in the blink of an eye, he could hear an entire opera. However, this phenomenon is distinct from the process of bringing something into existence in this visible world, such as writing a book or composing an opera. It is something else entirely. It cannot be achieved solely through inspiration; imagination is also required. By itself, inspiration is infertile and fruitless. We often think that imagination is useless, but it is the other great power within us. The power of inspiration is masculine, it represents our spiritual masculinity, regardless of our gender. Therefore, the sacred power of imagination is the feminine power within us, the holy virgin. We require our imagination to give form to the inspiration we receive from the higher worlds. Imagination is the mother to inspiration's father. Imagination must be the mother for there to be form. It must be the mother for us to effectively work with inspiration and accomplish something in this visible world.

Those two powers are inherent in creation and are always present. Thus, our physical manifestation as two distinct sexes is only a temporary phenomenon, as it contradicts nature. Instead of being solely male or female, we should be man-women, capable of creating without the help of another; that is part of our role as creators. However, we lack this ability because we are here to learn how to correctly use the creative powers of nature. This concept is intertwined with our division into two sexes, depicted with the sleep of Adam and the creation of Eve. It is preferable not to use the word "rib" in this context; a better and more accurate translation would be "side" or "other half." This better expresses that the hermaphrodite humans, originally created in the image of Elohim, were divided in two, so that each human being was now either male or female, having previously been both.

This division into two sexes is briefly portrayed in the creation story of Genesis, but the process of division naturally occurred over long periods of time. It did not happen abruptly, as depicted in Greek mythology where Zeus split humans in half, leaving each half to look for its counterpart. This is merely a metaphorical depiction of the events that unfolded over time. The division happened as one sex evolved and became more predominant in some individuals while the other sex became dominant in others. Following the example of animals, individuals began taking others as their mates. Consequently, one side, one gender diminished in an individual while the other gained prominence in their soul.

Thus occurred the division. Nevertheless, anyone who has studied these matters knows that today, the human being is physiologically hermaphroditic, even though the other half has atrophied from disuse.

Another thing which comes to mind when we think of the first origin of evil, is that all ancient traditions, such as Egyptian, Indian and foremost of all Greek mythology, which is very familiar to us, recount tales of strange creatures who are neither human nor animal, but rather man-animals, or animal-men. From Greek mythology we know names such as Fauns, Pans, Satyrs, Centaurs, Sphinxes, and various other creatures of forest or sea, who were said to have human heads but animal bodies, thus being half-human, half-animal. It is commonly assumed that these creatures were mere myths; that such creatures never really existed. However, we have to keep in mind that the original fall to sin involved humans following the example of animals, because they were, as the Secret Doctrine describes, amânasas, mindless. Humans did not understand to only approach their own species, thus also approaching animals. The animal-men were born from these crossings, for nature had not yet set any boundaries to breeding. Evidence of such creatures has been unearthed by natural scientists, who have discovered skeletons of what they have referred to as monkey-like creatures. These ancient tales are not without truth. A French researcher even posits that there is more truth in mythology than in history. Herodotus, the father of history, references instances of such animal-beings, half-animals, approaching human females. Greek literature mentions such singular incidents. It is plausible that such creatures existed in Europe relatively recently, and it could well be that they can still be found somewhere on Earth where scientists have yet not ventured. Alternatively, they may have already gone extinct, like the people of Tierra del Fuego, who faced extinction when white people arrived and – in a display of our praised "fine" manners – approached the local women with the consequence that all the women were suddenly rendered infertile, fruitless, and were no longer able to give birth. We Caucasians think it is "honorable" for us to have rendered another race extinct. Nature itself has set it so that there can be no more crossbreeding between the older races and the current ones, as well as between humans and animals. Individuals with perverted sexual inclinations may feel attraction towards animals, but such attraction no longer yields offspring. Nonetheless, this fall to sexual pleasure, lust, and desire, which occurred millions of years ago, laid the foundation for the rather tragic history of humanity. We must remember that sexual life is a difficult problem in the evolution of humanity. Every individual perceives it as their personal problem to resolve. However, for many, sexuality remains an insurmountable obstacle, because it is a profoundly influential power in the soul of humanity, and in the human body it causes difficult diseases. From this view, sexuality is a curse upon humanity.

However, the influence of evil did not cease when we humans came to know pleasure and all the inhuman, selfish filth it could lead to, but evil also rose to its peak through other means. While pleasure played a crucial role, additional factors contributed to the rise of evil. The rise of evil to its peak did not only require the subjugation of sensual pleasures but also the corruption of reason itself. The human reason, intellect, was contaminated millions of years ago in Atlantis, now lying in the depths of the Atlantic Ocean. Nearly all contemporary scientific researches believe in the existence of the continent of Atlantis, as described in ancient traditions. The ancient Atlantis of the tales, once inhabited by humanity, likely existed. Just recently, the papers wrote about an island that rose from the ocean on the American coast, and on that island, there were the ruins of a town. The island is currently under investigation. It may be that it once belonged to either Atlantis or Lemuria, another lost continent located in what is now the Pacific Ocean.

On this continent of Atlantis happened the strange tragedy, which caused our fall to true evil. The fall in Lemuria was a natural fall, but here in Atlantis occurred the fall to intellectual evil, true selfishness and wickedness, the tragedy which is referred to as black magic. We must not misunderstand that we, the current mankind, used to be great black magicians; we must not take this credit to ourselves, for a black magician is a highly developed being who controls great powers. We fell into black magic by becoming the servants of the black magicians out of blind desire and lust. We obeyed them and worshiped them. This raises the question: who were these black magicians? Last time we spoke about us being lured into pleasure, to experience all kinds of sexual life, by some kinds of beings within us. Those beings, who in this way became our seducers and tempters, were human beings from the old periods of creation, humans who had not yet attained that stage in evolution which was ordained for them. They are called by different names, for example, the Lucifers. These beings were the remaining beings of the Moon-Manvantara, permitted to possess us, yet they were inherently good beings. There were also human beings who were "repeating a grade", the Ahrimans. They were from an even older Manvantara, the Solar period. These beings told us that we cannot gain knowledge without studying the surrounding world, without going out of ourselves. They were also intrinsically good beings. Into Atlantis, into the most crude and coarse physical bodies, incarnated also beings from Saturn, the oldest incarnation of Earth, called the Asuras or the Satans. The Asuras were human beings, who were not inherently evil, but who now needed to gain experience of evil, selfishness, wickedness, cruelty, and pride. They needed to experience everything they had not experienced in Saturn, whether due to a lack of time or desire. Now the Asuras wanted to quickly experience evil, so that they could be purified of it in infinite suffering. They were not themselves evil; they only sought experience. The Asuras, or the Satans, came here to help us by tempting us. They incarnated in Atlantis and enthralled large numbers of us. They were marvelous, beautiful, powerful, and perfect ruler-beings, and they took us into their service and insisted that we worship them; they wanted to be our gods. We had already in an earlier period seen gods, been with gods, with them who had come to teach us in goodness.

They were Melchizedek and the members of his academy. We had served, followed, and admired them. However, these black ones, the Satans, wolves in sheep's clothing, demanded our admiration and service: "Kneel before us, or you will get hurt." We were like domesticated animals: when a cruel master appears, the animal must lick its master's hand, even though at the same time it might be building up vindictiveness within itself. Our relationship to these ruler-beings appearing in Atlantis was similar: they demanded servitude from us. We had to obey their commands, but at the same time they promised us rewards. They showed us all kinds of tricks and ceremonies that we could use to gain power over and enthrall the human beings we lusted after, those with whom we wanted to enjoy ourselves. Then they taught us to torment animals in a way that they would excrete sweat, bodily fluid, which could be then used for magical purposes and ceremonies.

Thus, cruelty developed in us and evil reached its peak. Those black ones taught us to use the creative power within us as intelligence and reason. Studying the human being in an occult way, we see that some of the creative power becomes sexual power, but some of it ascends to the brain as thought-power. We have learned to think with the help of the creative power. The black magicians taught us to think, but not to think unselfishly about higher affairs, but to think in a selfish and calculated way. They taught us to use our intelligence in the service of our lusts. Even now, many use their intelligence to satisfy their lusts and to get themselves what they need. However, we now also comprehend higher matters through our reason and thought. Back in Atlantis, the black magicians only taught us to use the creative power for selfish purposes. Thus developed our lower intellect and understanding, and so we ended up worshiping the Satans, the black beings. Note that the term "black" does not describe their appearance; they could have appeared in any hue. As we worshiped the black ones and their images, all kinds of malicious, mean, selfish, and cunning qualities developed in us, so that we humans really became somewhat lousy beings looking from our current viewpoint. Now we at least see good in all people; there is a divine being hidden within everyone; we see feelings of mercy and love in every being; but back then all this was very well hidden; our heart was becoming harder, malicious, and mean; we felt no mercy, we did not know much about love. Of course, there have always been exceptions.

This sad state of affairs led to the event called the heavenly war. By then, the leaders of our planet, the White Brotherhood, and all the wise beings had understood that humanity was going too far and sinking too deep into evil. Humanity must be saved, but a mere cataclysm is not enough; the humans themselves have to learn that they are heading the wrong way. Therefore, the first war in Heaven commenced. This war was not really fought in the invisible realms, but rather in this physical world. Perhaps this name "war in Heaven" comes from it being also waged in the air. All our divine sages and the great beings on Earth had unanimously decided that a war must be waged against the black ones and the troops they led: "Those human beings who wish to be in the service of the white ones come to our side, but those in service of the black ones stay there. Everyone must learn a substantial lesson." This war is discussed in all traditions, including the tale of "The War of the Sampo" in our Kalevala. Pohjola was a kingdom of darkness, but note that its name does not here refer to the northern countries, but on the contrary to the southern ones. The kingdom of Pohjola had stolen the Sampo, the key of all magical knowledge, the knowledge which was supposed to bring happiness to humanity, the knowledge of the hidden powers and abilities of nature. Those high black leaders, the Asuras, had stolen it, had brought it with them and turned it against all white knowledge. They had stolen the key of knowledge, the Sampo, and sealed it in a mountain, so that only those who wanted to serve their dark purposes could have access to it. Väinämöinen, Ilmarinen, and Lemminkäinen – the white forces – decided to set off to get back the Sampo, and they rallied all their troops and a terrible war began in Atlantis. This war was fought mainly in the air with airships, but also on the ground. It naturally served as a substantial lesson to all humanity. In this war the high leaders of the black ones and great numbers of the human beings serving them were annihilated; some were taken as prisoners and others killed.

So was vanquished the rule of the black ones. However, defeating the evil powers was not enough. Humanity was so tainted that nature itself had to intervene; Atlantis had to be eradicated by a natural cataclysm. Plato mentioned the island of Poseidon near Gibraltar that was the last remnant of Atlantis, but it too sank into the depths of the ocean during the last deluge. Before that the white forces had moved their own troops towards East, towards Asia, and this is described in the tale of Noah.

This was the first remarkable war in Heaven, and from then on there has lived an idea as an axiom in the consciousness of our mankind. This axiom says that when oppression becomes too great, holy war must be waged for a sacred and just cause against evil. Since then, war has become ingrained in humanity's consciousness as a sacred institution. The fight to defend one's Fatherland or religion is often perceived as holy. Therefore, in this fifth root-race we notice how war is deemed great in all old tales, how only someone who dies as a hero in war is a real man. We cannot even question how this inner belief in war has managed to live to this day as a great and moral concept, for this teaching originated from a high authority.

We must now also discuss yet another heavenly war. The external, physical war waged in this visible illusory world by the true white sages, the troops of Melchizedek, was only meant as a metaphor. It was like a magical gesture in this visible world, for even they knew that true war could not be waged here, for war would only destroy that which is innocent. Everything created here on Earth is innocent; fields, cities, meadows. The human body is also innocent as it was originally created as a temple for the Holy Spirit. The war in this visible world is merely a metaphor, a reflection, a magical manifestation of the true war, which is something completely different. Even the White Brotherhood, if we dare to say so, was somewhat amazed by the ethical impact and profound impression this teaching made on the consciousness of humanity, leading people to believe that this war must be fought here in the visible world. Therefore, the Brotherhood waited a long time for Christ, this human, who would be able to bring truth into this world allowing Him to conclusively state: no more war or violence in this world.

However, we must understand – so as not to become self-appointed judges in our narrow-mindedness – that the first lesson we have learned from this great moral struggle remains the grandest moral act in humanity's consciousness.

What then is the second war, the true battle the white sages tried to teach us about? It is a war that can be called the war in Heaven, because it takes place in the invisible realm, the astral world. What war is this? It is the battle against one's own evil, against one's bad habits, malice, and lust. This is the only true and inevitable war. Since the time of Atlantis, it has been waged with the White Brothers and all the sages at its helm. All who have heard their voices or the voices of their emissaries have been called to join an invisible army, where every individual fights against the evil in themselves.

This second heavenly war is such a remarkable thing that the holy books called its participators righteous and just. By no means does this army include the whole of humanity.

It is peculiar that William Booth came up with the name "Salvation Army", for in the invisible world there is such an army, even though the recruits of the latter army fight against the evil in themselves. No one can be recruited into this army unless they are fully committed to fighting against the bad tendencies in themselves. This army has grown quite large in numbers during the course of hundreds of millions of years, even though compared to the whole of humanity it is still relatively small. This army is remarkable, for its members are called righteous and just, and it has the potential to achieve more than we can imagine throughout history. There is a tale in the Old Testament, where God said that the towns of Sodom and Gomorrah would be spared if there are even fifty righteous people to be found. With dread, Abraham had to answer that there might not be fifty righteous people around: everybody just worshiped their own selfishness and self-indulgence. God then asked whether there were ten or even just five righteous ones, but there was only one righteous man, Lot, who was forced to flee the town. If there had been more by his side the towns would have been saved. Why so? Because the battle these righteous ones wage against the evil in themselves is in itself an unfathomably great moral factor in the world. The matter is not limited to one fighting against the evil in oneself: at the same time one fights against the evil in the society. For example, the city of Helsinki has its own astral atmosphere, aura, to which all the thoughts and feelings of its inhabitants rise. Those feelings may often appear selfish and animalistic, but if righteous people fight against evil, they also fight against the terrors of this aura. Therefore, when there are enough righteous people in a town, it needs not to be devastated. The consequence of evil, sin, is death; it is a natural law that any place that has too much evil in it must be eradicated by cataclysm or war. Too much evil cannot be allowed to come into the world. When we humans bring forth too much evil into the world, we at the same time sow the seeds of the destruction of the world. We human beings destroy each other in our madness, and natural catastrophes wipe out one place after another from the face of the planet. This is the law of life. We must not be like animals anymore, neither should we be black magicians. We are human beings; we are called to be human beings. God does not prevent us from being evil, but karma will bring the consequences, for we have broken against the law of life and it says to us: "You must be good, perfect." Our evil actions will have consequences and these consequences will destroy us. Therefore, righteous people help by obliterating evil from the atmosphere of their domicile. They also act in this visible world, demonstrating goodness through their example and helping humanity advance. As a result, humanity is now more advanced than it was a hundred thousand years ago. However, even now it is often asked in the secret councils of the gods: "Do righteous people exist?" Such councils were held often during the time of the World War, and when the answer was "No," the judgment befell. Still, there are examples showing that good is achievable. During the Great Strike of 1905 in Finland, there was the potential for bloodshed. However, miraculously, a sense of righteousness and belief in the greater good prevailed, thus preventing violence. 12 years later, in 1917, as the challenges of the global revolution were being felt here in Finland, the question arose: could bloodshed be averted once more? Could this nation maintain its purity through the ordeal? Regrettably, at that time, there was insufficient righteousness, faith, goodness, and trust remaining to prevent the violence that ensued.

It is incredibly important for a nation or a town to have enough righteous people. Nothing bad can happen to those righteous ones themselves, but more importantly they are able to help mankind. Let us remember: the Secret Brotherhood, the sacred fraternity of Melchizedek, cannot interfere with the history and development of humanity in any way that would affect humanity's karma. It is our responsibility to save humanity by cultivating holy and righteous people within our own community. Most of the members of the White Brotherhood are already from our mankind, but there are not nearly enough of them for them to be able to in any way support this enormous mass of people on Earth. If there are 60 billion people attending the school on this planet, that is a lot compared to the few thousand of those who belong to the White Brotherhood. People often blame the Masters for allowing so much evil to happen, without taking into account that the job is absolutely overwhelming and of legendary scale. We do not know how much love, self-sacrifice, and mercy they have. This small group is relatively powerless compared to the formidable multitude of souls in humanity. We must cultivate righteous individuals among humanity to change human history. This is the purpose of the second war in Heaven, which has been fought from the times of Atlantis.

V

WILL LIGHT WIN?

The still ongoing third war in Heaven was initiated by Jesus Christ, with Gautama Buddha having prepared it beforehand. To comprehend the nature of this war, which we are all called to wage in Christ's name with His aid, we must study those ancient times in Atlantis, preceding the first war in Heaven.

As we recall, the first war in Heaven was a great war between the white ones and the black ones in Atlantis. Even though it was a corporeal war, it mainly took place in the air. Perhaps this is what earned it the name heavenly war. The second heavenly war, as we remember, was fought in the invisible world in the sign of the Old Covenant. To understand the third war, the war of the New Covenant, we need to examine those times in Atlantis and remind ourselves of the kinds of human beings – or, if we prefer, human-angels and god-beings – there were in Atlantis, along with the influences we humans received from each other and the nature of our own beings. Although we have previously spoken of this, it is still good to revisit these facts again as we turn our attention to this third heavenly war.

We now turn our gaze towards the late Atlantean times, just before the great war. What kinds of beings had incarnated into Atlantis?

Firstly, starting from the top, there were those wise, initiated teachers who had founded the Secret Academy on our planet. Those teachers had come from elsewhere; they were not part of our mankind. They were perfect, divine, and wise beings.

Secondly, there were those mysterious Satan-beings, or Asura-beings, who had incarnated into Atlantis. They were human beings from the distant past who had not reached the ultimate perfection offered to them in their own evolutionary era, or Manvantara, in the first incarnation of our planet, the Saturn-incarnation. Those marvelous Asura-beings, Satan-beings, just needed concrete experience of evil and the potential of selfishness to be able to attain the same wisdom their human brethren had attained in that distant past.

Thirdly, in Atlantis, we find those spectacular, wise human beings who also came from a different incarnation of our planet, from the distant ancient era of the so-called Sun-Manvantara. These beings are called the Ahrimans. They were highly evolved, wise humans who still needed to gain more experience before they could reach the same wisdom their more evolved brothers had attained in the Sun-Manvantara. They needed the experience of goodness and the experience of devoutness and illusion. Just as the Satans had to experience black magic, or evil will, in order to understand the good will, or white magic, the Ahrimans had to experience illusion, but also the devoutness of feelings, the complete surrender to emotion, to be able to gain a true and clear understanding of the true nature of feelings. These were the Ahrimans.

Fourthly, there were in Atlantis those peculiar beings we call Lucifer-beings, Lucifer-spirits, or just Lucifers. These beings are the humans who had not reached the human perfection available to them in the previous incarnation of our planet, the Moon-Manvantara. These Lucifers are those human beings from the Moon who had been left behind. However, when we study the Secret Doctrine, we notice that it uses the name Lucifer in a somewhat broader sense, even though it presents these matters in a slightly vague manner. They're presented clearly, but also at the same time covertly, so comprehending all this is actually really difficult unless you are previously acquainted with these matters. When you read the Secret Doctrine, you notice that it is a very complicated work especially when it is explaining these things. However, when we take heed of all the references presented in the book, and also of our own experiences and observations, especially our occult observations, we can reasonably assume that the category of Lucifers does not only include those human beings who belonged to the mankind of the Moon-Manvantara who are now destined to obtain experience in this incarnation of Earth through the current mankind, but also all those human selves who were not part of the mankind of the Moon-Manvantara but instead belonged to our current mankind born from the animal kingdom. Therefore, we can call Lucifers those beings, commonly known as fallen angels, who refused to incarnate immediately due to their reason and their capacity for judgment.

I have previously tried to explain how one-third of all human selves refused to immediately incarnate on Earth. Two-thirds of the human selves incarnated right away into those original physical human bodies, but one-third refused to incarnate at the same time. They said they wanted to wait. The Secret Doctrine emphasizes that their desire to wait stemmed from pity. They felt that it would have been futile for them to be born into humanity at that time, akin to attending the first grade in school after having already passed the fifth grade. Therefore, they wanted to wait for humanity to reach a higher grade before incarnating. This is how the humans, who were born as human beings in the Moon-Manvantara and who belonged to our mankind, felt. They constituted one-third of the human souls, as mentioned in the Apocalypse. It is also stated in the Apocalypse that when Satan fell from Heaven, he took with him one-third of the stars in the sky, referring to those human souls. Who was this Satan who tempted others to follow him? This Satan was composed of those Lucifer-beings, who had been human beings for a long, long time, belonging to the mankind of the Moon-Manvantara, and thus, were infinitely wiser than the newborn human selves. Nonetheless, these newborn human selves were intelligent due to their varied experiences and the influence of those Lucifer-beings. If I interpret what H.P.B. hints at correctly, we can categorize all these humans who belonged to the mankind in the Moon-Manvantara, as well as the humans who had been born from the animal kingdom, as Lucifer. Thus, the term Lucifer encompasses not only the actual Lucifer-spirits but also one-third of the human souls, or the selfhoods of our mankind. Together, they all belong to the kingdom of Lucifer.

Let us now imagine that all of us sitting here were souls from the group that had been born as humans in the Moon-Manvantara. Back then, we all were Lucifer-beings and we followed the suggestion of the actual Lucifers: "Let us not be born into humanity yet, to that first grade, but let us wait for humanity to evolve, and then we shall be born." However, not everyone on this planet is a Lucifer-being, nor does every single human being here belong to the kingdom of Lucifer. I have discussed the old Masonic tradition which teaches that mankind can be divided into two large sections. All human souls are either Abel-souls or Cain-souls. The Abel-souls make up the majority of humanity. They are the quiet, content souls who uphold this life, and are naturally more obedient and peaceful. Without the Abel-souls, there would be no life. The Cain-souls, on the other hand, are lively, intelligent, somewhat discontented, revolutionary, and restless. Simply put, all the geniuses of humanity are Cain-souls. The Cain-souls are the Lucifer-spirits. They are Lucifers. The Abel-souls, however, are the souls who were born as human selves on the Moon during a later period or here on Earth. That is in no way a negative thing. Jesus said, "The first shall be last, and the last first." The same wages are paid both to those who came late for work and those who came early. There is nothing bad about the majority of souls having been born as humans a little later than others. On the contrary, the others have a more difficult karma because they have had more time to do evil; they have more to struggle with and more to overcome. They must overcome a lot of what is unnatural and useless, but their struggle is balanced by their great ability to have mercy and to love.

All these beings lived in Atlantis. Thus, in humanity, there were both those obedient souls, who were immediately born when the human bodies were finished in this Manvantara, and also the Lucifers who belonged to Moon's mankind and were left behind in the Moon-Manvantara. The Lucifers aided the undeveloped human souls by possessing them. They did not incarnate into physical bodies, but instead they invaded the souls and the feelings of others, and figuratively lit the spark of intelligence in them. However, in the beginning, the spark naturally drew them downwards rather than upwards. Those naive human souls did not understand what was happening to them. The pre-existing spark of reason was ignited to action by the Lucifers, who had a constant influence over the young souls, and thus, the young human beings fell to sin. This was the first great Fall to sin. The creative power started to have an influence on human beings, and at first, it mainly flowed downwards as sexual power. However, when humanity was divided into two sexes, the creative power split in two. While still a part of the creative power coursed down as the sexual power, now part of it could also flow up as the internal creative power, the thought-power.

The Cain-beings of our mankind awaited in heavens until they got their opportunity to be born. We must not think that those actual Lucifer-beings of the Moon-Manvantara, who had to "repeat a grade", would have quickly gained experience through those relatively simple humans and then have been immediately liberated. No, they also remained here, and some of them still exist even to this day. They actually ended up in a similar position as the other human Lucifer-beings; they had not incarnated as human beings, yet they were close to humans. Let us think about ourselves. The whole of humanity as such has now become so intelligent and reasonable – with some minor differences between different races – that all people can now be said to be somewhat Luciferic. A certain self, a Higher Self, has formed within all human beings, and this Higher Self is Lucifer. The name Lucifer stands for "the bringer of light." If we receive an occult experience of our true self, we come in touch with our Higher Self, which is its own separate being on the mental plane, i.e., the world of intelligence. Every experienced person knows this from their own experience. Here, a human is a personal being, yet they can still connect with their Higher Self, which is distinct from their personality. The Higher Self is the Lucifer in an individual; it is the Bringer of Light in them. Our Higher Self is so separate from us that we can, if we find ourselves in an ecstatic state or if we happen to be clairvoyant, perceive our Higher Self as a completely separate being, and we can in this lower consciousness even have a conversation with it, and yet, it is our own spirit. We can move into it leaving behind our personality. When our consciousness leaves our physical personality – I wish to mention this so that we do not get any unwanted ideas about the name "Lucifer" – and moves without any division into our Higher Self, Lucifer, we have a divine experience. In our Higher self, we are remarkable, high, wise, and marvelous beings, without any feelings of superiority, without being prideful in any way. In this state, we are such wise and marvelous beings, that when we look at our physical body and think about the personality which manifests in it, we say to ourselves: "How is it possible that I am bound to this being, which is so greatly ignorant, dark, and black? How can I, a human being, who belongs to a wholly different world, a god among gods, be bound to this being who knows nothing?" One experiences this when their personal consciousness joins their Higher Self. Then one really gets to know their true self. In this state, one is distinct from the physical personality familiar to us, yet still aware of being forced to live in this physical personality, and almost feels sad about their fate. As a Lucifer-being, one lives in a wonderful world of inspiration, truth, beauty, and purity, and here on Earth one knows very well the nature of that fallen angel. A human being is a fallen angel, descended into physical life with a grand and wonderful purpose; to redeem one of these personalities and, at the same time, redeem matter in general; all this for the purpose of helping others. One is aware of this in their Higher Self, and one also knows that Lucifer is the Bringer of Light. In their Higher Self, one is also aware that they themselves wanted their personality to attend the school of the knowledge of good and evil. Without attending the school of the knowledge of evil, there can be no knowledge of good. Therefore, this is one of those psychological and metaphysical problems we only understand when we experience it ourselves.

Among us there are such Lucifer-beings, who actually belong to the mankind of the Moon-Manvantara, but who have adopted a physical personality in this current mankind. There are also the Lucifers, who originally belonged to the newborn mankind of the Moon-era, but now are known as our Higher Self. There are also groups of undeveloped human beings in yet undeveloped races. Even in our own races there are undeveloped humans, whose Higher Self is still young and weak. Even though their Lucifer-aspect is still weak, they are still Lucifer-beings because they have a reincarnating Higher Self. They are referred to as the Abel-humans and they are naturally obedient and receptive to teaching. However, the actual Lucifer-beings, the Cain-beings, feel it is their responsibility to teach humanity. Every intelligent person feels that. Our whole society in civilized countries is built on the principle that people need an intellectual upbringing. What else are our schools for? Of course, it is now beginning to be understood that schools should also be cultivating character. However, education remains focused, and will be even more focused, on cultivating intelligence, since we also hold the idea that character cannot develop without intellect. We are prone to think that ignorance and goodness are linked, but we also intuitively feel that goodness should be associated with intelligence. Because intelligence is what is usually missing from people, we naturally want to cultivate it in others and in ourselves. Therefore, we are Lucifers, or bringers of light, in the sense that we try to cultivate intelligence and reason in ourselves and in others. Our whole culture and civilization is based on the cultivation of intelligence, and on the most powerful beings pushing the rest of humanity forwards with all sorts of inventions and scientific accomplishments, and also with art, religion and philosophy. We are raising a new humanity by every means possible, and we do this based on our natural instinct. We understand culture as something innate; it comes instinctively from within.

Now let us remember: there were all these kinds of beings in Atlantis. When we look at the first war between the white ones and the black ones, we see how humanity was divided: others sided with the black ones, others with the white ones. How is this to be understood? We see that the wise teachers, who had come from elsewhere, acted as the leaders of the white ones, with almost all the Ahrimans siding with them. The Ahrimans did, however, tempt our mankind to evil by proliferating from themselves, via their aura, the desire for experience and adventure, the desire to feel, for we do, in fact, experience life through our feelings. As Schiller said, "What you feel belongs to you, what you think belongs to everybody." By spreading to us the desire to feel, the Ahrimans drew us outwards; us, the primitive groups of people, whom the high Lucifers were influencing by suggestion and possession. We humans gained from these Lucifers the inner voice which told us: "Rise, rise upwards, the real life is within you; real pleasure is in what you feel within." The inner voice said: "You must learn to know the evil within yourself, you must learn to know pleasure and all that which is good in life, and all of this is found within yourself." However, at the same time, the Ahrimans around us drew our attention outwards, out of ourselves. The Ahrimans told us: "You cannot experience anything within yourself unless you experience the outer life." Thus, the attention of humanity was drawn out into the external life, and our humanity fell into sin. At the same time, humans felt the pain of all suffering.

The Ahrimans, who had striven for good, quickly understood the teaching of the wise ones: "The real adventure, the real experience, is that by cultivating yourself, you conquer the forces of nature and gain power over this visible nature." The Ahrimans easily understood this. Therefore, they did not seek the experience of life our humanity sought, but instead they remained pure and followed the instructions of these wise teachers. They had to learn strange yoga, spectacularly opulent magic. Obeying the white ones, the Ahrimans practiced this yoga, and thus were able to rise and gain the experience they needed. They were able to leave our mankind behind, and they no longer really exist. Their spirit, which they embedded into humanity, still remains. It is a powerful spirit, an adventurous spirit striving for knowledge, without which our humanity would not get along. This spirit is a great factor in our quest to conquer this planet and nature. We have a strong desire for experience and adventure, and this desire is especially prominent here in the Western culture. This spirit is the Ahrimans' gift to us, but it is also a deceptive force in our spiritual life as it draws our attention to the external, away from our own spirit. It draws us to only seek the truth outside of ourselves and from the surrounding nature, so we cannot see the other path which is also necessary to us. The Ahrimans themselves, as personal beings, broke free from our mankind. Similarly, the Satans, or Asuras, who had tempted us into black magic in Atlantis, also escaped.

The white ones, as I mentioned earlier, won over the Ahrimans to their side. However, they did not just win over the Ahrimans; they also won over human beings; both a great number of those human beings from the Moon, the actual Lucifers, and also a great number of undeveloped human beings from our mankind. The black magicians won to their side a very large part of our humanity and a great number of other humans, who did not really understand much of anything. This great division took place in Atlantis, and one side lost this war.

Now a question arises: How were the white sages able to assist humanity following the great catastrophes, particularly now, after the emergence of the fifth human race? How were they able to help humanity during the era of the so-called Old Covenant? Of course, the great masses of human beings could not be helped much, for their reason and intelligence needed to evolve naturally. There were always teachers and religions around, but those great masses could not really be helped in any significant way. We had almost instinctively followed the black magicians in Atlantis. We had worshiped them, and we had been very enthusiastic about being able to have all the pleasure we could want. Following the great catastrophes, we were born into new races. We were left to evolve naturally, but what about those beings who were already more evolved? How did the wise ones try to help them? How did the White Brotherhood try to help the Lucifer-beings?

I will right away state one thing, an axiom, which everyone who has done any introspection knows to be true. There is within us, via Lucifer, via our intelligence, two great potentials for evil, which are apt at preventing our spiritual progression.

One of these potentials for evil is the Mephistophelian characteristic of doubt that our intelligence acquired from the Ahrimans; our intelligence will not believe anything, it wants to experience everything first hand. This doubt is a great hindrance to goodness. We are prone to doubt. It is a great weakness, unless we turn it into a strength.

Another great weakness, another potential for evil – unless we overcome it – is our ambition and pride. Because we are reasonable, intelligent, and genial beings, we notice that we radiate pride and gladly rise above others. We are ambitious. We want to be competent in the eyes of the world, but more accurately we want to be competent in our own eyes. We are doubting and proud by our nature. We are proud because of our Lucifer-nature and doubting because of our Ahriman-nature, because of the spirit we received from the Ahrimans. Our Lucifer-nature makes us so arrogant, that we would even storm Heaven.

As we know, there is but one way by which we can overcome suspicion, distrust, and pride, and that way is love. Let us think: if we truly love another person – I am not talking about any sensual ecstasy – we come to trust them. When we love someone, all this Ahrimanic distrust fades away. As much as we love, as much we trust. When we love another person, we do not stand proud before them, but instead we humble ourselves. We want to be absolutely humble, for love is the act where we give up the desire for power and ambition, and instead humbly offer ourselves to the person we love. This is familiar to us from our everyday experience. The same behavior can also manifest in sensual love: a man can fall on his knees before his loved one, if his greatest happiness in the world is to get this other person. This is of course a caricature of the way humility manifests, but it is analogous how it manifests in true love. I do not say that it is not an act of true love when a man falls on his knees, or that true love could not also be manifested in external humility. When we love, we trust, and in this way, we free ourselves of our distrust and pride, which are obstacles to our spiritual development.

The old wise ones had to inspire trust and love in us. Not sensual love, of course, but true love. Because these Masters and Teachers are primarily found in the Eastern lands, we can, when studying the Eastern conditions in the past and also in the present, notice how a Master, a wise sage, takes an apprentice or a student only after having become convinced of the student's trust and love. Back then, if a person sought the truth or the path, if they desired spiritual evolution, and if they had heard about a teacher, they would request admission to study under the teacher. Of course, such a person who strives to find a teacher is actually seeking spiritual evolution. During the times of the Old Covenant such search was very rare; there were not many people who sought the truth.

If you read stories about the old sages and yogis of India, you learn that when a student aspired to study under a sage, the sage would always initially reject the aspirant. The teacher perhaps refused to see the student altogether. The first time the student came around, the teacher might have been surrounded by his other students, completely ignoring the new aspirant. Perhaps the other students pushed the aspirant aside. This was the first trial. "Why do you come to me?" The teacher received the aspirant coldly the first time, refusing to see him: he wanted to test whether the aspirant returned. If the student became overcome by disappointment, he did not return, but if he had true desire, he did return. Perhaps on his second attempt he got to meet the teacher. The teacher asked the aspirant: "What is it you are looking for? Why do you come to me?" The student, of course, prostrated himself or bowed deeply and explained that he had experienced such and such dreams and visions; he had studied and become absolutely convinced that this was his teacher. "If you have studied a lot, then you must be competent. Why would you then need to come to me? Do not seek anything from me, just go to others." Thus said the teacher and so the aspirant left once more. This was the second test. Then, perhaps a year later, the aspirant returned for the third time. He still insisted that he could not go to anyone else and that he only wanted to study under this teacher. He felt that only this Master could help him. "Well, if you really are crazy enough to think that, can you then endure the ordeals I will put you in? For I think you are insane. Perhaps I will place you in a dark cave where you will stay for many months." "I will endure all," responds the aspirant, "if I just can be your student." When the aspirant finally became the teacher's student, seven years passed filled with the most horrifying experiences, during which the teacher tested the aspirant's love and trust. The aspirant was treated absolutely coldheartedly. The teacher tested him, for example, by saying, "I feel unfathomable lust towards a woman who is getting married soon. Bring her to me." Without any hesitation, the student embarked on the trip. Of course, he got beaten up at the wedding, and he returned crawling, saddened, to his teacher to tell him about the misfortunes he had faced. The teacher smiled and said, "Do you think I really needed that woman? Now go away and tend to your wounds." After seven years of trials the aspirant was initiated as a true student of the Master. Aspirants had to face such ordeals during the Old Covenant. That was the only way to bring forth the trust and love in them. Otherwise, they would not have been purified of selfishness and everything bad. This system of the Old Covenant is still largely in use. Now, of course, the student in this terrible school on Earth also belongs to the army in another world. This army is the one that enacts the heavenly war I spoke of last time.

I see that I did not really get to the third war – the one initiated by the Buddha and commenced by Jesus Christ – but I will say a few things as an introduction. The constant goal and the constant question of the whole White Brotherhood was: "How could we get the divine love, Christ's love, into this physical world, the visible world, so that it would be available to all humans without the requirement of those drastic preparations and efforts there had been so far?"

They knew that such a thing was possible only if that divine love itself, the divine life, the perfect love, physically manifested on Earth. If the archetype of love, the image of God, the image of divine love, comes into this visible world, all people are bought and redeemed in their souls, and the road to salvation opens up to everyone. However, the Secret Brotherhood knew that this great work could only be accomplished if a human being from our mankind lets God take him, so that Christ, Adam Kadmon, the Son of God, could fully manifest in him. This was the sole prophecy of the White Brotherhood. They awaited and prepared for it, for there were a few Lucifer-beings from our humanity — not those people who were left behind in the Moon-Manvantara — who promised them that they would redeem humanity. There were two foremost of all, who gave this promise; the one who became Gautama Buddha, and the one who became Jesus of Nazareth.

These two initiated the third heavenly war.

VI

LUCIFER AND ANTICHRIST

The third war in heavens began, as we have said, by the work of Jesus Christ. It is still ongoing, an eternal war waged by humanity that will inevitably end in humanity's victory. To understand this war, we want to observe it from three points of view, while always referring back to those other heavenly wars we have previously talked about. The three points of view I want to examine regarding this war of Christ are: firstly, the question of evil in general and the types of evil we must overcome in each war; secondly, the question of the Karmic Atom, which we explore to comprehend both the work of Jesus Christ and His war; and thirdly, the question of the divinity of Jesus Christ in comparison to all the other earlier and later helpers and redeemers of humanity.

The first question is the question of evil: what is the nature and essence of evil; that which evil is in itself? I believe that it is not difficult to define evil in a universally applicable way. I think of evil as a phenomenon, as a reality; not only as the inner ethical reality, of which we have spoken a lot and which is generally regarded as the actual form of evil. However, we do not believe that evil is solely the subjective and natural evil of an individual at the human stage of evolution. Instead, we view evil as a natural phenomenon, a cosmic reality. For in all times, there has been a belief that, alongside the subjective evil, there exists a kind of evil in nature and the cosmos that can befall a living being. What is evil in this significance? It is death and loss. When we think that the sole, deepest essence of existence is life – its fundamental essence is life itself – we understand that evil is that which offends life. Evil is what cuts it off in some way, what prevents it. From an objective standpoint, evil is the inhibitor of life, its destroyer, death. Hence, it is called the final enemy. We must remember that in life itself, in divinity, there is no evil, for there is no death in divinity. Therefore, in the most profound sense, there is no evil. However, in manifestation, in all manifested reality, there is this potential for life to end, the possibility of loss. That is the so-called objective evil. It is a completely separate matter that from our perspective, this objective evil may not be perceived as evil, but rather as good. Let us take an example: if we have a disease, we say that the disease is evil. If we have cancer in our stomach and it bothers us terribly, we want to get rid of it. So, we let a doctor operate on it. However, if we take the viewpoint of the cancer, then the operation is its death, the end of its life: what is evil to the cancer is good to us. That is a very blatant example, but in our existence, the objective evil is death, the death of forms. The form makes judgments, turns good and evil into relative concepts, and perceives everything from its own point of view. It defines something as evil and wants this evil to cease and disappear; it judges good and evil in relative terms.

An individual, who is under a sin, engaging in sinful behavior, may mistake the evil of the sin for good, as it brings them pleasure. However, sin inevitably leads to suffering.

Later, the individual realizes that this evil behavior is not anything good afterall. Evil does not only bring forth bodily suffering but it also inhibits us as humans, as free beings, from rising to those spiritual heights we wish to attain. The evil of the sin might have seemed good before, but now it has become a sin; now the individual wants to be free of it. Is the evil of the sin happy about this turn of events? Has the sin already become a habit? How does the sin feel when the individual says that it must now die?

When I look at this world from an occult point of view with my inner eye, I see that nothing is purely subjective, everything is objective. Evil and sin are objective realities. Evil is what bothers us; it is like a parasitic plant or a devilish being, distressing us. It is like a great battery of power constantly begging us to feed it: "Give me life or I will die". It is one of our sins or vices saying this to us. There is nothing in the thoughts or imagination of human beings that could simply vanish into nothingness. We cannot say that if we do no evil, then it would do no harm to sometimes think selfish or sinful thoughts: what impact could mere imagination have? In this way people comfort themselves, but in this they are wrong, for there is nothing which is nonexistent. There is nothing which is purely subjective, but everything is objective and real in its own world. Therefore, our evil tendencies are objective; they exist as such. Overcoming them and labeling them as evil is an unpleasant death sentence to them and they will fight for their lives. This is a very important aspect to understand in all psychology.

When we consider the evolution of man and all three of these different wars, we remember that the first war was that which began in Atlantis when the white magicians defeated the black magicians, saving us from the excessive temptation of black magic. What is black magic? Black magic is something that can influence our will, turning it black. What does it mean that our will turns black? It means that our will knowingly goes against the will of God. What does this mean in practice? At first, it means that our will becomes cruel, causing us to want to cause suffering unto others and to torment and harass others and do all kinds of evil. We can already see the minute tendencies of the black magicians in children. Unbeknownst to the children, they may have inherited these tendencies from Atlantis through their bloodline. These traits mainly appear in little boys – not so much in girls – who kill flies, tormenting them by plucking off their wings and legs. Children do this quite unknowingly, yet this behavior is an old inheritance of black magic, capable of either growing or vanishing. Cruelty is the first step into black magic, whether it be manifested in deeds or thoughts. This cruelty is soon revealed in war and in everything which is connected to it. During war, people forget their humanity and they can end up in an indescribably cruel state, as if in a trance. If an individual participates in war, they fall under mass hypnosis, mass suggestion. War, of course, already being black work in itself.

This white war against the black magicians in Atlantis was absolutely necessary to save the young human soul. Why was it necessary? To understand this, we have to observe the state of us human beings at that time. We had already been born as humans millions of years earlier, but we were still quite young and in our selfhoods we were still on the heavenly plane, which is the home of the human selves. When we incarnated into our physical bodies, our selfhoods – those tiny fluttering flames – and this tiny thought, or reason, grew as the centuries passed. However, the black magicians secretly began to tempt the young human beings into worshiping them, not because they wanted to harm the humans, but because they wanted to evolve themselves. The experience they needed could have become extremely fateful for us if they had managed to awaken in the tiny, childish self a black will, the cruelty of will, the selfishness of will. This would have been extremely fatal for us, as it would have resulted in death. This death, our departure from the heavenly state, would not align with the will of nature, the will of life. Death cannot occur without one's awareness; it only happens through the conscious choice to become a black magician, leading to moral self-destruction, and spiritual and metaphysical separation from the Monad. This cannot happen for there is but one Majesty and God. No human being can die, no divine being going through the human phase can die, but only the one who wants it. Who wants it? Only a few want it and the willing then disappear, but even they do not go away for eternity, for they must once begin a new life. There is nothing else but life. However, an individual can choose to give up their immortality and die for an unfathomably long time. That is the fate of the black magician who sets their will against life.

The black magicians of Atlantis sought to tempt us, beings of lower intelligence, yet such actions are prohibited on behalf of life. The white ones fought this great war against the black ones to protect our selfhoods from them for once and for all. They set protective walls around our selves. In this way was organized Heaven, the paradise the human selves can only leave by choice. The human selves took the form of an angelic kingdom, a hierarchy in the invisible world. All these human selves are protected, and they are all in God's care. They must not be tempted away. The angels of each one of us are in Heaven, and like little children, they have turned their gaze to God. They will no longer fall into black magic.

This first war in Heaven, the great war of light against darkness yielded a great result. We must thank the White Brotherhood, this original group which came from elsewhere, for their great help. Their work still continues; the Brotherhood has recruited great numbers of troops, they still protect the human selves as a wall against evil, for it is the will of life. However, the help we received as young child-beings was not a show of mercy on behalf of the White Brotherhood, it was not an act of goodness and self-sacrifice towards us, but rather it was the command of nature, the will of God. The more we grow, the more we feel gratitude for those who still take part in this work, and we ourselves hurry to participate in it.

The second heavenly war is the one human individuals wage, following the example and prompt of the White Brotherhood. The first war is referred to as the war against Satan, or the war against evil will. The second war takes place in the human soul. It is the war against Ahriman, who tempts us susceptible human beings to succumb to all the feelings and sensations which bring us pleasure, joy, cheer, and personal happiness. At the same time, we are prone to abhor the feelings which limit or disrupt peace. In our emotional life, we seek in our the feeling that could remain and be eternal; the feeling in which we could always live without the disruption of inner peace and harmony. This we seek, but we are then under the great illusions of Ahriman. The illusions lead us to believe that this feeling is good. They suggest that only within it will we find peace and happiness.

Ahriman wields a special weapon which allures us and makes us kneel before it; this weapon is beauty. Feeling lures us by its beauty, and we fall prey to all kinds of emotions. Within ourselves we know that we seek something that could free us from all the so-called feelings, all sentimentalism, and all deceptive piety. We seek something that could give us the permanent and eternal feeling of peace, that would let us eternally stay before our master, God.

During the second war in Heaven, the White Brotherhood helped us by teaching us the prerequisites for eternal happiness and how this happiness can be achieved. All their teachings point in the same direction. They say: "You must strive for everything pure, for truth, love, nobility, and unselfishness, to eventually reach the true undying feeling. All other feelings are subject to death."

We do not want to live in a feeling that is destined to die, but in one that is permanent. Therefore, every young person dreams of great love, eternally beautiful, enchanting, and pure. A young person does not believe that their sensual affection and love should be allowed to fly around. No one admires Don Juan or Casanova. No young woman idolizes a woman like Lucretia or Messalina. A young woman cannot relate to a public woman who, at one moment, loves one person, and at another moment, someone else. Instead, the young woman wants to feel true love towards her friend. This rarely happens, but we are getting closer to the time when a true woman finds a true man and vice versa. Even though this dream is not yet reality, it can still give some solace to the human soul. Only a few will experience this, for the emotional life is flickering. Feelings change. The fact that we as humans even understand to yearn for a more permanent feeling is the achievement of these teachers. They have tried to teach us the nature of true emotion and that the reward of sin is death: "Do not yield to pleasures, for they are followed by suffering." It is the law of causality that there can be no pleasure without suffering. This law is difficult to avoid, but the great teachers have always tried to teach liberation from these fluctuations of the polarities, so that our soul can travel along the horizontal line, leaving all the disturbances on the surface. We must attain the equilibrium of the soul.

When people in the old times sought to follow a teacher, they often chose to leave this visible life behind in order to be free from the opposites it causes. The ancient Indian society was organized in the way where at a certain age one was entitled to leave behind the everyday life. When one had served as a youth, gained an heir as a man, one could then retreat into meditation. There were also people who from a young age were allowed to leave the company of others and freely to develop the powers of the soul; they could freely leave this visible body and in another world attain equilibrium, so that no pleasure could lure them nor could any suffering frighten them. However, most people lived ordinary lives and only accepted a few pieces of good advice. The advice helped everyday societal life to progressively become more and more human. The still ongoing second heavenly war is fought in the invisible world against the desire hidden in the human soul to chase rainbows, to pursue illusory goals. This is the fight against Ahriman.

Although we are now being overly descriptive to make our point clear, we must not forget how all these different aspects are mixed in a human being. Nevertheless, when we describe this subject, we notice that at different times of history, attention has been drawn to its various aspects.

In the first war that took place in Atlantis, the focus was on the fight against Satan and the triumph of the white ones, although it was not yet the triumph of us human beings, who were merely protected. In this second war the focus was on the fight against Ahriman. The teachers urge us to follow them.

Now we come to the third war, the war of Christ, fought predominantly against Lucifer. Christ defeats Lucifer and commands us to fight against him. Lucifer is close to us human beings; in fact, he is our Higher Self. Christ does not fight against Lucifer, but against the personal self he represents; without Lucifer we would not have the personal self, the Kama-Manas. The war of Christ is the war against the evil that is not only within our astral side, but also deep within our personal self. What is the evil in our personal self? We could say that it has two forms, but in reality, it is just one form manifested in two different ways: evil manifests in us as vainglory, as our arrogant pride in our ability to judge, and as the supposed inner knowledge of the nature of true happiness, as our pride in our supposed knowledge of how everything should be. Arrogantly we judge God's work, pointing out the things that are wrong. We can even go so far that we say that there is nothing divine and nothing moral, only blind forces of nature. We become materialists, believing our reason – which we have obtained as a result of a long process of evolution – is the highest. We start to believe there can be nothing higher than us. We appoint ourselves as the final judges in this universe; we can determine what is ugly and what is beautiful; we are the ultimate arbiters. In the end, we cynically laugh at the mere thought of the existence of goodness or love. We have reached the epitome of wisdom; there is no God, nothing like such. Or, we have become skeptics or agnostics who think that nothing can be known and who laugh at all knowledge. If, for example, there comes a sage, saying that he has experience, and he tries to teach us about sin and the wage of sin – which is death – we arrogantly laugh and say: "Oh, how can a man be so blind that he thinks he can know something? There is no knowledge; everything is uncertain, illusory, and vain. There is no other knowledge than that which can be studied scientifically."

If we still hold an agnostic or materialistic stance, we are still in some way undeveloped. We must acknowledge that even though scientists can tell this and that, in the end we do not know anything. Only God knows the true nature of everything. Research tells us that there exist plenty of things, and as crazy as it sounds, who knows, maybe God exists too. This we must admit as modern people. Despite this, because we can precisely experience the level of modern research, we may in our prideful ignorance think that the scope of knowledge ends at a certain point. Just like a former school headmaster says: "I have a degree of Master of Sciences; I know everything there is to know. What I do not know is no longer any real knowledge." Many may fall into such stupidity. It is our ignorance and pride which comes from within, inflating itself within us, because our self is aware of us being gods. Therefore, our Lower Self can bloat like a frog that wants to inflate itself to the size of a bull.

We believe deep within ourselves, that our sexuality is the real basis of all life and happiness, and that without sexuality there is no charm, happiness, or sweetness to life. We believe that the whole allure of existence comes from sexuality. Therefore, we think: "If I could just find the one I could truly love, if there only was someone I really liked, then what else could I care about anymore? If there was someone with whom I could form the whole cosmos, the whole world, I would no longer need anything else." This belief is very deep within us. Even if one says that true happiness and eternal peace can only be found in God, one could still hold on to the idea – even after a lot of experience and suffering – that if one could just find true love, one would be happy. Due to our pride, we cannot with our reason and thoughts define eternal bliss and happiness. We should free ourselves of this pride. Of course, I am not implying that you have not noticed this about yourself already. Rather, I'm saying that we must engage in proper introspection to detect any remnants of that arrogant belief within us, for our pride comes before a fall. Our pride must be vanquished and we must come to the conclusion that things should not be arranged according to our will, but rather according to the will of the Father, the will of life itself. Whatever life wants in regard to our happiness and bliss, we will no longer complain, for we know that life has prepared for us such things we cannot foresee. Eternal life is behind everything. It might be unforeseen great love: millions of people will be able to love one another. We will be able to love the whole of humanity, and we will no longer yearn for anything personal, anything small. Life might hold great surprises in store for us. There are people who have suffered much and become so lonely, that they have told themselves that they do not believe in any wonderful love, but they can still love everybody and be good to everyone. This is something all wise ones and those who have overcome their pride know, and pride cannot interfere with it.

This is what Jesus accomplished with the third war. He defeated Lucifer. He tried in his own life to set an example, to give this life to us, so that we could receive the peace of Christ, the happiness of Christ, that could stay with us even if everything else was taken from us. I do not mean that we have become intolerable here on Earth. No, the more we live in Christ, the more this Earth will become a paradise. If we live in Christ, we become free from our selfish yearnings and our life on Earth becomes indescribably happy.

VII

BY WHOSE HELP – OUR OWN?

It is said in the New Testament: "Ye are bought with a price, therefore be not the slaves of men." These words "ye are bought with a price" refer to the great secrets of our human evolutionary history. It is possible that they refer to all three aspects of the secrets, for this "redemption", or "buying with a price", is in relation to the three heavenly wars we have been discussing. Regardless of whether the New Testament only refers to the last war – the one initiated by Jesus Christ – or all three, the phrase "ye are bought with a price" is a beautiful and fitting description of all these wars and their achievements.

We have discussed these wars before, emphasizing that to understand the third heavenly war specifically, we need to study this matter and these heavenly wars from two points of view. We previously explored these wars in relation to the problem of evil and death, and how they pertain to overcoming death. However, this same question of overcoming death takes us to the next question, or viewpoint, from which we wish to study these wars. It is the viewpoint said to be in connection with the Karmic Atom, and the question regarding the divinity of Jesus Christ.

Firstly, we would like to direct our attention to the question of the atom: what is this Karmic atom that we have received? To understand this, we must briefly focus on the question of the essence of the human spirit: what is the essence of the human being? We all know that the entire ancient Theosophical wisdom, revealed in all religions and true philosophies of the world, teaches that the human being, in essence, is a child of divinity, a son of God. Human beings are divine, born of God, born of the great secret of life. Essentially, the human being is a spirit, and as such, is also God. The human being is not merely a pile of matter, not a heap of atoms, not a body living and dying and finally vanishing into nothingness. Human is not the form; human is the spirit. This is true spiritualism, and it is the opposite of all materialism. Therefore, since the beginning, the Theosophical movement has fought against materialism.

In our time, it is no longer in accordance with the latest scientific achievements to adopt a materialistic stance regarding the great questions of life. On the contrary, our greatest scientists and thinkers acknowledge that spirit does not merely result from matter, but exists independently. Spirit, or consciousness, is the aspect of existence that is closest and most familiar to us, for we are conscious beings. Without consciousness, we would know nothing. From the spiritual standpoint, spirit is something existent, as eternal and ancient as matter. Spiritualism does in no way deny the reality of matter, nor does it adopt the extreme stance of denying the existence of matter. Spiritualism says that matter does not exist any more than spirit does, for only God, divine life, is behind everything perceivable. We perceive only the manifestation of this divine life, with its two sides; spirit and matter. It would be ridiculous for us to deny either side. Spiritualism teaches us to understand matter. Matter is not only what we understand as forms; it is not merely a collection of physical atoms.

When we look at this visible world, we say that it is made of atoms. What are these atoms? Our scientific thinkers say that the secret of the atom cannot be solved. As they delve deeper into the study of the atom, they observe that it may merely be an assumed point in space, a vortex of power with unknown origins that generates what is perceived as physical atoms. An atom in itself is a secret, a power capable of containing within it reason, thought, anything, as ancient wisdom tells us. The perennial wisdom has always wanted to say: this atom, or more accurately this matter is God's magical power. It is nonessential how we wish to describe it, for all descriptions are mere words. We cannot figure out the secret of the atom, but this matter can be made clearer when we think that within God Himself, within life itself, hides a secret power by which life – the secret potential – can manifest. Manifestation is directly dependent on the limitation of this limitless, infinite life. As spiritualists, we preferably want to understand this boundless life as consciousness. Limitation is born in this boundless and infinite consciousness, and it is dependent on the secret of matter. However, let us not forget that we cannot comprehend the absolute limitless consciousness that has no object. The limitless consciousness, or the absolute life, appears to us as unconsciousness, and therefore, we do not want to define it. When the magical power of matter causes limitation in the manifestation of life, regardless of its mathematical size, consciousness emerges. This consciousness, emerging when matter imposed limitations on life, is itself limited and can become aware, conscious of itself. Boundless infinity without any limitation cannot become conscious because it is consciousness itself, and thus, unconsciousness. Consciousness exists only in manifestation, and in manifestation, there is limitation and form. This is an old philosophical, esoteric point of view. The foundation of matter, the inner essence within divinity, lies in its capacity for limitation, through which consciousness is manifested.

This is the philosophical background, the most profound secret of all existence, but it does not provide us with a practical explanation for our manifested cosmos. Therefore, we must further inspect manifestation and limitation. What more can we learn about them? The first awakening to manifestation and limitation, representing the first limitation of life, occurs within the Father. The first true manifestation unfolds within the Father, within the first unmanifested Logos. The most profound metaphysical reality of manifestation is the Father's continual begetting within His timeless infinity. All old religions and esoteric philosophies teach that this Father is love, the essence of love. As we know, love is not merely a passive emotion or state but is instead defined by the active expression of love. Without something to love, love itself lacks substance and significance. Therefore, the essence of love requires something that it can love. As old Indian philosophy teaches, the love of the Father is characterized by the fact that He multiplies and divides Himself. The Father loves all this division, all those beings born of Him. These individuals, who are born of the Father, are called Monads, or sons of God. These Monads are singular units of consciousness, as perfect as the Father Himself.

However, love is not limited to the acts of begetting and loving. Rather, its essence is infinite bliss. When those individuals, who are loved by love itself, loved by the Father, reciprocate with love, they themselves become blissful in it and gain the ability to love, and thus they can reach the infinite bliss that is the essence of love. The love of these Monads, or sons of God, towards the Father is initially rooted in their innate knowledge of his love, rather than in any self-aware ability to love. As Leibnitz said, these sons of God do not yet possess the true ability to love; this ability is based on the self-awareness of the being. The self-aware being is an individual capable of love. How can these Monads, sons of God, acquire an individual self – a selfhood, an essence of consciousness capable of love – as soon as they are born? They cannot simply be born with it, for it is not something innate.

All love is based on freedom. True love is always based on us being free beings. We know from our individual human experience that it is not love when a blind force of nature, a sexual force, enthralls us and pairs us with another person. That kind of sexual attraction is merely a force of nature. Love is born when this force of nature pairs us with the right person, or when we ourselves understand its lesson. Love can be born in a couple when one of them becomes a mother, giving birth to a child: then love for the child is born in both of them. The child cannot yet consciously love its parents back, but is still in a mysterious way a joy to them. Nevertheless, the parents feel unspeakable love, compassion towards the little one: they would not be able to abandon it. In some religions, children have been abandoned, but this has not been apt at developing human emotions. Small baby girls have been left to die on fields because boys were wanted.

However, we have to turn a blind eye to this for now. The coming of a child into the world is such a wonderful mystery that it teaches the parents to love. It is the first school of love, but this first school of love also includes the time of the pregnancy: when the woman becomes helpless, the man takes care of her. He observes the woman becoming a mother with compassion, and thus learns renouncement and love. Later, the child teaches the parents to love. When all enchantment disappears and beauty fades away, the couple is stripped bare, what is left is a friend, a companion to love. And love awakens and grows. There does not always need to be a child. Sometimes these people are already a bit more evolved, and can perhaps learn the lesson of love without a child. Either way, in a true marriage two people are learning to love one another; they are not just enthralled by the blind force of nature. They learn to value and trust each other. What could be sweeter than this triumph of love, this birth of love in the hearts of two people? The ability of love, the potential of love, is hidden within every person, but only in the school of experiences can a person truly learn to love. Love is the result of the manifold phases of life.

The example of parental love helps us understand the situation of the Monads, those pristine spirits, the sons of God, who are born from the bosom of the Father. The Father loves them, but they cannot yet love him back. They receive the Father's love like little children receive their parents', especially their mother's love, but they cannot reciprocate that love, they cannot yet love one another. Therefore, the school of life, the great manifestation of the cosmos, the manifestation of the universe, teaches these sons of God, or Monads, to love. This is no minor lesson, no quick achievement, but one of millions of years. We humans, who now are taking our first steps in learning love, free love, have already gone through fabulous periods of evolution to get here. We are just now starting to learn the lesson of love. Love must be free and aware; an individual must know and feel their own love; they must love consciously. For this reason, the great play of creation exists. It is a school of experience for the pristine spirits. What is this school of existence, this great adventure of existence like? Is it random, without any program or plan, or is it well-organized, well-measured, and well-drawn beforehand? It is well-organized, as testified by the experience of all sages and proven by all ancient knowledge. Every one of us can learn to experience this. Our cosmos is well-organized and our evolutionary history is wisely planned beforehand. What has been given to us for aid? What has been given to these Monads, spirits, sons of God to guide and protect them? This is where the atom, the magical power of matter comes in. When the Father begins the process of manifestation, He first begets within Himself a perfect image of the objective that must be attained: the image of the perfect Son of God, the human being. This great, perfect, heavenly human, the image of God, lives in the consciousness of the Father. It is the second Logos created by the Father, the Son born from Him in a different sense than the earlier Monads. We must note that the Father, as a consciousness, emanates these sons of God, Monads, yet simultaneously within Himself, within His consciousness, He creates the image of the perfect man, the perfect Son of God. We call this image the Cosmic Christ. It is not the same as all these Monads, sons of God, who are also born of the Father. The Cosmic Christ is a synthetic image. However, this image, the Cosmic Christ, does encompass all the Monads. We must add another thing, the most important one: the Cosmic Christ is the lamb sacrificed since the beginning of the world. The Cosmic Christ is a material manifestation, because He is an image. Naturally, our languages and words are more or less metaphorical and clumsy, so we cannot accurately describe the divine with human language. However, this perfect image of the heavenly man, the living image, is at the same time the secret of matter, because it is the first form of manifestation. Those singular units of consciousness, sons of God, Monads, are not proper forms; they are like drops in the ocean, simultaneously one with the ocean; they are like sparks of a fire, one with the fire. They are not limited by form, until they receive form from the Cosmic Christ.

Now, I would like to briefly describe things like this: each Monad receives an atom from the body of the Cosmic Christ, from His form. Each Monad becomes a Monad, an individual, by joining an atom of the body of the Cosmic Christ.

I have tried to describe these things analytically, even the things that perhaps should not be analyzed because they are closely related. Yet, it would be wrong to say that these Monads, sons of God, these individuals, are strictly speaking merely atoms in the body of the Cosmic Christ – they are not – because they are also God's only begotten children, monogenēs, born of the Father, as described in the New Testament. They are more like brothers of the Cosmic Christ, but even that is not the correct way to phrase it. They are born of the Father, but they have also joined an atom in the body of the Cosmic Christ. The Cosmic Christ is one with these atoms to such an extent that we cannot make a distinction here. When we view reality metaphysically, all we see is the great, heavenly Son of God, Adam Kadmon, whose body encompasses and includes all the Monads. His body is seemingly composed of an infinite number of glowing stars and each of these stars is a Monad. Only when we inspect the Monads more closely, we see that their manifestation, their material aspect, makes up an atom in the body of the Cosmic Christ. However, as units of consciousness, the Monads are born of the Father.

This is the great metaphysical background to all manifestation. Our task is not to follow the evolution of this manifestation, its descent into matter, or its further descension lower and lower. We will not continue following the wondrous journey of the Monads through all the natural kingdoms, as it does not pertain to our evolution. Instead, we now focus on the point in time during which the physical manifestation of the human being on this planet takes place. We have now come to humanity and have seen that behind every human being there is a star, a Monad. This glowing, bright star is an atom in the body of the Cosmic Christ. Reaching the human stage is already a great achievement in itself: the human being is a self-aware, conscious being of reason, that has already started to manifest its inner spirit, the Monad, in some way.

The self was born within the human, and in these lectures, we have traced its evolution and phases in connection with the problem of evil in those great spectacles known as the heavenly wars. The first war took place in Atlantis, where the White Brotherhood performed a grand beneficent act for the good of humanity. We can now briefly touch on this help given by the Brotherhood, which came from elsewhere. Let us examine how this great redemption connects to the teaching of the atom, our Christ-atom.

When the human self was born into its own heavenly world, the first help the self received from the White Brotherhood was that they protected the self from black magic, from the dominance of evil. The human self was too naive and inexperienced to be able to resist the temptations of evil; hence, it needed help. The act of falling into black magic must be a deliberate choice made willingly by the individual, rather than being influenced by enchantment or temptation. The human self needed to be protected from this. That is why the White Brotherhood saved our selfhoods from this danger in this first war. The Brotherhood held us in a protective heavenly sphere, in which it still protects the little child-selves. Another way to put it would be to say that this refers to the atoms in the body of the Cosmic Christ, which enclosed us within themselves, embodying our spirits, our Monads. The atoms were originally in their unfathomably high, heavenly world, not a physical locality but rather an inner, spiritual, moral world. The White Brotherhood helped these atoms to descend to the level of selfhood and to imprint on every human self a seal, an image of the perfect, heavenly human. Based on their previous experience, the Brotherhood recognized this image, and its implications for the reasoning and thinking self. They knew how to place this seal on the human self.

The atom of the body of the Cosmic Christ hidden in the human self is the great protector of humanity. It allows the human self to be instinctively and consciously aware of its objective: its mission in life is to know the path of evolution. The work of the White Brotherhood – which, in the physical world, focused especially on the war against the black ones – has given us the image of the Son of God, the knowledge of our divine origin and paradise. Our Higher

Self would not have been able to aspire to the connection of the inner spirit on its own. Instead, the image of God, or the awareness of us being the sons of God, was imprinted onto our selfhoods millions of years ago by the Brotherhood. Think what a grand work, what an important achievement this was! The birth of the self prevents us from accessing our higher, inner spirit, where the innate image of God lives. Therefore, the self stays small and childlike. Our self, which cannot access our higher spirit, did not know anything about the Son of God, His perfection, or the human objective. Only through the imprinting of the image of God onto our human self did it become aware of its own objective. You can read in the Secret Doctrine, in the part where it tells about the work of the Manasaputras and about the help of the White Brotherhood, that this impression took place when the White Brotherhood joined the atom to the selfhood.

Now you, without a doubt, notice how clumsy our language is when I talk about the atom. We think that the atom is tiny, but in reality, it is nothing like that. The atom, which I am referring to, is the image of God within us, yet it also holds a material secret. It has a form, it gives form to our consciousness. Therefore, I call it the atom.

Now then, when we think about the second heavenly war, we make the following observation: This atom, this image of God, was drawn even further downwards into the human personality, or the astral body. However, this transfer of the image of God, or the atom, from the self to the personality could not occur the same way as the initial impression. Instead, sages and wise teachers, ready to sacrifice themselves for the good of humanity, were required. This group included all the members of the White Brotherhood, who had come from elsewhere, as well as the new human recruits — those wise human beings who had chosen to sacrifice themselves for the sake of humanity. These sages have helped us by being our teachers and examples. They have traveled among humans since the dawn of time, appearing every now and then. Throughout history, wise beings have emerged within humanity, sacrificing themselves for others in this material world filled with endless amounts of distractions that often lead us to forget our true nature. These teachers have always reminded us of our nature and purpose. They are the great moral and spiritual teachers, who teach us to purify our emotions. Human beings inherited from the animal kingdom the natural disposition for pleasure. As we humans have lived in the sensory world, we have developed our skills to such an unrestricted level, that it has led us to consciously seek pleasure. These teachers have always tried to teach us: "Do not indulge in pleasure, vice, and sin. Understand who you are; seek more sacred feelings in your emotional life. Do not degenerate yourself to sensual beings, but develop soulful, spiritual emotions within yourselves. Know that the most beautiful feeling on Earth is faithful love. Do not seek pleasure, but learn to serve others and to find happiness in friendship and cooperation."

This is what the wise ones have always taught us. They have waged the second great war in the invisible world, and they have taught us to purify our astral body, to develop within it the higher and more beautiful attributes. Some of us have been able to astrally evolve, but others have not been able to do so. There are several hundreds of millions of souls on this planet, but only around ten million of them have managed to evolve by internally purifying themselves, and now they, in the inner, astral world of their souls, participate in this second heavenly war against sin and vice, fighting for everything good and just. With the help of their teachers, they are helping the image of God, the atom, descend into the astral world, into the emotional body. First, the wise teachers helped them to receive the atom into themselves, into their own astral bodies. The presence of these teachers and their disciples has caused their light to shine in the invisible world, to shine on humanity, allowing us to see how this atom, the image of God has descended into humanity, into humanity's astral nature, its emotional body. Most people are generally unaware of this phenomenon and also of the image of God imprinted onto our self. However, in the course of millennia, those who have heard the voice of the teachers, have left to seek teachers, as they used to say in old India. They soon felt within themselves the yearning for more pure and sublime emotions, which helped them purify their own astral bodies. In the visible world, they have comprehended the human perfection, and they have even become able to see the heavenly human, Christ.

Those who have followed the path of the great teachers, have evolved beyond their consciousness. In another world, they learn to perceive the heavenly human, Christ. After acquiring this ability, they await His coming in the visible world. However, before attaining this capability, they were unaware of how to bring Christ into this visible world. Here, within their own personalities, they only knew that they must strive towards the perfection exemplified by their teachers. After seeing Christ, they felt within themselves the new moral, purifying powers, and they saw how much they had progressed. However, this progression has often taken the form of them retreating from amongst humans. They have become hermits, ascetics, working in solitude; they have become occultists, mystics who, in the invisible world, aid humanity through their thoughts and feelings. This path is still open today, and some people choose to follow it.

We can say that whereas the first war in heaven and the initial help provided by the White Brotherhood removed death from our self – for falling into black magic would have led to death – this second war removed death in the invisible world. The second war cultivates the awareness that allows an individual to continue existing as a self-aware being after the physical death, with the potential to be reborn into the world while remembering their previous existence. This has been how immortality, the overcoming of death, has been understood for hundreds of thousands of years. The East gives us a great example of this idea. You have all read about how in Tibet there are two head Lamas; Dalai Lama and Tashi Lama. If the Dalai Lama is the more political, external ruler, then the Tashi Lama is the inner ruler, the "pope". You have also read that a Lama is always a reincarnation of the same spirit, the same human individual. Whenever a Lama nears his death, he tells his closest friends that he will soon die, and then be reborn as a child. He tells them the signs by which they can recognize the child. The friends of the Lama often have to travel to distant villages looking for the child. Usually, they take with them some belongings of the old Lama, like a rosary, a tea cup and other similar items as well. When they finally find this child – who can be a week, a month, or even a year old already – they bring before the child all those items they brought with them. As a sign of the child being the reborn old Lama, the child unerringly chooses the objects which belonged to the old Lama. The child also has to say a certain phrase.

We have the most intriguing accounts of this phenomenon, which are not mere fairytales, dating back to the time of Marco Polo, from everyone who has reached Tibet. Even these days, there are such accounts by some researchers, who have witnessed this phenomenon. They all admit having stood amazed before this mystery without being able to understand it. These irrefutable accounts testify that the spirit of the old Lama is now reborn as a child. Thus, the same mysterious, evolved human being always sits on the throne. Sven Hedin, a Swedish traveler, got to meet and photograph the Tashi Lama a few years ago, and he said that it was the most profound, wonderful experience of his life. He did not anticipate finding something so sweet as the Tashi Lama on Earth. His expressions exuded kindness, radiating love, his words were imbued with wisdom, and his knowledge was extensive. Despite his youth, his presence was absolutely incredible. "I can never forget him", wrote Hedin. Hedin did not theorize about it, but his little story reinforces the faith shared by everyone in Tibet that the Tashi Lamas and the Dalai Lamas are the reincarnations of their respective spirits.

I mentioned this anecdote because it is a descriptive example of how one can overcome death in the afterlife. Because will is in immediate contact with the physical world, one can attain an immortal, self-aware personality in the invisible world and be born here over and over again. This victory over death is the highest achievement of the second heavenly war.

Now we come to the third heavenly war, the redemption performed by Jesus Christ, and its connection to the atom. As I said, the White Brotherhood has awaited since the dawn of time, or at least since the second war, for the human who could bring the image of God, the atom of the body of Christ, into the physical world and into the physical body. This long-awaited event marks the third milestone in overcoming death, signifying not only the achievement of immortality in the invisible world but also the overcoming of this visible world and the attainment of immortality in all worlds. An individual is no longer required to be born again, but unlike the Buddha, they do not have to stay in Nirvana or on its threshold. Instead, the individual can become the master of both the visible and invisible worlds, fully overcoming death. One has only one body, which is both visible and invisible. The body is the atom of the body of Christ, enlivened by the individual. This immortality is the achievement of Jesus Christ. Jesus gave us a metaphor: "A treasure, a pearl, is hidden in a field. When a man heard of the pearl, he went and sold everything he had to buy that field." This depicts the secret of our physical life after the coming of Christ. Jesus Christ caused this atom to descend into this physical world, into His own body. He fully embodied the Son of God, the image of God. He became the Cosmic Christ here on Earth. His atom, His cosmic Christ-self, was now able to shine on the whole of humanity, conveying the image of God, the atom, into everyone. Through the work of Jesus Christ, the pearl – the seed of perfection, the Son of God – is now in the physical being of every one of us, in our hearts. Therefore, Jesus Christ opened up a totally new path. He revolutionized our relationship with the kingdom of God. He said: "Now is the kingdom of God among you, now is the kingdom of God near. Change your minds, enter now the kingdom of God, you all have the potential to reach it in your physical daily consciousness." Most people do not know about this; they do not feel that they have this precious pearl in their physical bodies; they cannot believe in it. However, it is close to everyone, closer than ever before.

This is the third redemption, the final peak of redemption, the third aspect, which the New Testament refers to when it says, "Ye are bought with a price." Through Jesus Christ completing His mission, the Cosmic Christ was able descend into this visible humanity. Now Christ is at the door of our hearts. Before, Christ existed only in the invisible world. To many people, Christ is still more easily understandable in that way. Many are called, few are chosen. However, at least to the called, the chosen, there is the possibility to come in contact with the Cosmic Christ in the physical daily consciousness. This means that we can in our physical daily consciousness evolve to perceive the perfection of the Son of God, the human perfection, our goal and mission. All this takes is a change of mind, a conversion. When we convert and change our minds, we can comprehend the reason for our existence; we can see the perfection of the Son of God, the image of God, in our daily consciousness. Then we can begin to work towards fulfilling it; then we feel the power of the Cosmic Christ descending into us with the help of Jesus Christ. We are then no longer unsafe, lonely, and left on our own. We cannot achieve anything solely through our own power; rather, it is through the power of the redeemer within us that we can accomplish. This is the experience which is now available for everybody, possible for everybody.

VIII

THE ANTICHRIST

The secret of the human spirit is truly profound, for within it is not only concealed the secret of spirit or consciousness, but also the secret of form and matter. We say that the human spirit is the only begotten son of God the Father, a Monad born of the Father. The conscious aspect of the spirit is joined with the material and formal aspect which is the potential for the manifestation of matter. We call this material aspect of the human spirit the image of God, the divine seed, and the secret of matter. I have also referred to this material aspect as the atom. The idea of the atom is inseparably connected to this idea of consciousness. Together, consciousness and the atom constitute the human spirit. As previously mentioned, we should not interpret this term solely in its physical and coarse meaning. The atom is the sole secret, the potential for manifestation. This atom is inseparably linked with spirit, or consciousness. We also describe the atom as the divine Mother, born of God and born by God. Therefore, it is also the same as the body of Christ, as the Father and the Mother together give birth to the Son, the perfect human, the ideal of existence in the consciousness of Father God. Because it must also possess a form in order to project any manifestation, it must be coupled with the idea of matter, or the Mother of God. Thus, the Son of God is not only the thought of the Father, but also the image of the thought of the Father – the form given by the Mother.

These profound metaphysical problems are difficult to comprehend logically. However, once we experience the Son of God, we also experience the Father and Mother of God.

As we mentioned last time, the image of God in the human spirit is also an atom in the body of Christ. It has existed within our spirit since the dawn of time, and following Theosophical custom, we refer to it as Buddhi. This atom, the image of God, the spirit, is Atmâ-Buddhi, and only in it is Manas born, as the result of a long evolution. The manifestation Manas seemed distant; it appeared as a reflection in the entire manifested world. However, when the human, Manas, is born, the potential for the immediate manifestation of Atmâ-Buddhi emerges. This Atmâ-Manas is initially born as the thinker, the self, outside the image of God. Therefore, as I attempted to explain last time, the first guidance given to human selves is the same assistance we received when the White Brotherhood came here and established their secret academy. They enlivened and electrified this atom, allowing the image of God to be imprinted onto the consciousness of our selfhoods, to enter the consciousness of our Higher Self. However, it occurred instinctively, not with self-awareness. Since then, our selfhoods have been aware of the image of God, the ideal of perfection, in their own worlds. Every person is vaguely aware of the perfect human, the objective of life in their Higher Self. This Higher Self, which does not appear immediately at the beginning of human evolution, must be protected to prevent black magicians from luring it to death. The Higher Self must be preserved.

The White Brotherhood erected a protective wall around our Higher Self, ensuring its focus remains solely on goodness and the objective of life, shielding it from all other influences. If we experience our Higher Self, we notice that it does not know evil, and only wants good. The White Brotherhood has helped our personal self, the physical reflection of our Higher Self. In the astral world, which is the spirit world closest to our consciousness, the Brotherhood has taught us, as it has taught for centuries and millennia, to aspire for goodness and truth and to raise ourselves. They have caused the image of God to descend into the Astral world; but, even then, not everyone became aware of it. Only those who followed the great teachers, and who became free of their bodies, were able to see the heavenly man, Christ, and aspire to his union. Those who did not begin to earnestly and devoutly follow the great teachers, but instead lived shallow and worldly lives, did not become aware of the image of God – neither in this visible world, in their daily consciousness, in the spirit world, nor even in the soul world.

The third milestone in human evolution occurred when Jesus Christ came into the world and completed his mission. He brought the image of God into the physical world, into the physical human. The image of God is now alive in all of humanity. However, it cannot be assumed that everyone is aware of this. We notice that it is absolutely necessary for most people to first follow the old teachers, to become aware of the image of God in their souls, in the invisible world. They cannot see Christ in their daily consciousness, unless they have first seen Him in their souls. To become aware of this image of God in their physical daily consciousness, most people still need to first see the living image of God imprinted onto their souls in the spirit world.

We must not misunderstand that the atom was at the level of Buddhi, somewhere really high in touch with Atmâ, or that the atom was first transferred to the level of the Higher Self by the White Brotherhood, and that from there it was moved to the astral level by the great teachers, until it was finally brought to the physical level by Jesus Christ. It did not happen like that. This atom, which is the image of God and the secret and idea of matter, is also, simultaneously, a physical atom. It is the human magical power invigorating this world. There is only one kind of an atom; let us not dwell on tiny physical atoms, but rather think of the image of God, which forms the basis and foundation of this physical world. This atom has also been called the permanent atom and the Karmic atom. In its occult sense it is a physical atom, or an etheric atom, a whirl of power, but, since the beginning, it has existed on all these different levels, without humans being aware of it. However, the human spirit, Atmâ, has always been fully aware of this Buddhi, this atom, whereas our self only became aware of it in the manner we have described. It is like the atom was energized through the different stages of consciousness of the human spirit. The image of God came into to the consciousness through these different stages. The atom itself has always existed.

Why is this matter so important to understand from both the ethical and occult standpoints? Because, otherwise, there would be no absolute temple of God, temple of the Holy Spirit, in a human being. There would be no absolute divine support and safety in the personal self, no absolute divine origin. There must be a support, an assurance of safety and security, which is embodied in the image of God, the human atom. This atom is present in the body of every one of us, and the human body is always built in accordance with it. Therefore, the human body is an extraordinary gift to us; better than what we ourselves are. Our bodies are more evolved than we are: the body is like our older brother, our teacher in the temple of the Holy Spirit. Death is inevitable when we live in error and sin because this atom revolts against us. When we give into vice and sin we negatively influence the atom's vibration. It does vibrate at first, but eventually it rebels against us: "I can no longer vibrate in all this error and sin, in all this vice. I will now revolt and destroy this temple." This causes our death. The atom revolts even if one has already begun to raise oneself in the invisible world but still sins, falls into wrong emotions, or assumes wrong opinions. The atom cannot endure this and dies. However, we humans have the eternal flexibility and evolutionary power of the image of God. We are not lost, but bought with a price, because at the beginning of time, we received the image of God, the image of the Mother of God, which is the Christ in the human body, and because we have been helped multiple times to become aware of who we are and where we shall go. The teaching of the New Testament is correct when St. Paul asserts, "Through sin, death came into the world." We are unable to avoid committing sin because we are in the school of evolution and we need to attain the self-awareness present in our spirit, Atmâ, though not yet realized in our Manas, our humanity. This awareness of God must be attained in the long school of life. Thus, we eat from the tree of the knowledge of good and evil and commit sin and fall. While it is a necessary experience, it is nevertheless a school of death: through this school, comes death. All the help we have received has been aimed at ensuring that we do not lose our way, guiding us to stay on course toward our goal without veering too far in the wrong direction.

At first, we were protected from the toils of the black magicians, the Satans, then we were taught how to be wary of the great temptations and illusions of the Ahrimans, and finally we were taught how we can protect ourselves from the Lucifers. And now we are here. Jesus Christ has helped us for the third time, and His help has been like a summary of all the other help we have received. He has, as it is said in the New Testament, come to the world to overcome the Devil. Jesus Christ has gathered in Himself all the potential for overcoming evil and has made it possible for us to ascend to God. Therefore, Jesus Christ is essential to us, essential to our entire history of evolution. St. John correctly said, "There is a spirit of the instigator, spirit of the Antichrist, which opposes the work of Christ". What is this spirit of the Antichrist? As John the Apostle described, the spirit of the Antichrist is "the one who does not acknowledge Jesus Christ, who does not acknowledge the Son, who does not acknowledge that Jesus Christ is God." This is the first important definition for the spirit of the Antichrist, and soon we will get another definition. The spirit of the Antichrist, which opposes Christ, is that we do not acknowledge Jesus Christ as the incarnate God, and that we do not acknowledge the divinity of Jesus Christ.

A seeker of truth might find it peculiar that, after enduring several agonies of the soul, they come to the conclusion that Jesus of Nazareth was human, bringing peace to their soul. The concept of Jesus Christ being God was nothing new in Christian thought, but seeing that Jesus Christ is also human, and could thus understand the seeker a little, gives solace to them. The seeker then wonders, whether it's still correct to say that Jesus was God? It is very important and natural for the seeker of truth to go through these steps of learning. Every individual must go through the same process, for the awareness of Jesus Chris being God does not come from baptism, not from the confirmation school, not from churches, not from sitting and listening; it only comes after the soul has experienced great agony and turmoil. However, it can only come after we have first understood that Jesus of Nazareth is human. When we understand His humanity, we can also understand His divinity. The fact that He is God means that He brought God on Earth. He revealed to us God the Father. He said, "Whoever sees Me, sees the Father, for the Father is love, and I am love; who sees Me, sees love." Jesus Christ, from a young age, by no means knew that He was the God of the universe. At first, He only knew that He was a human being like everyone else, albeit in a different way. But after His baptism at the river Jordan, He understood that He was God, the Son of God, and one with His Father. He was filled with the great love of the universe, which He could manifest to the great masses who were largely unaware of it. People are not very aware of the love behind all life. They come up with all kinds of ideas about divinity. For example, they might invent a great group of gods with different attributes, quarreling gods, or great and powerful gods, and so on. People can have diverse ideas about God, about the great force behind life, about life itself, but only Jesus Christ brought us God, the highest God we know, the God we call love. Jesus Christ is fully aware of this love.

We must not think that we are entitled to analyze the emotional life of Jesus Christ, as is often done, and ask questions such as, "Was He aware of His own divinity?" After getting baptized, Jesus Christ became aware of His own divinity. Before His baptism, Jesus could be discussed as a psychological phenomenon, but afterward, He was completely enveloped by the great love of the universe. He became able to declare, "Look at Me, and you shall see the Father." This we notice from the own words of Jesus, "I and the Father are one. I am in the Father and the Father in Me; I do what Father commands and what Father does." There is also the strange passage that has caused much disapproval: when speaking about a sheepfold, Jesus said, "I am the door. Only through Me does one go to the Father," and thus to eternal life.

Does this statement from Jesus imply that he has renounced all the earlier teachers and redeemers? Are they now considered meaningless and false? Not at all. "I am the door; I have always been the door; all the great prophets before Me have always referred to Me. If you understand them correctly, they have all traveled through Me in the invisible world, but none of them have yet brought Me into this visible world. They have always, in the invisible world, led to Me, who am the door. Now the door is here, for I am here." In Hebrew, the word for door is "ptah". It is also the same in Aramaic, the language spoken by Jesus. "Ptah" is simultaneously an ancient Egyptian name of God. When Jesus says, "I am ptah," He might be implying, "I am God." There is even more to this word "ptah" which is composed of the three consonants P, T, and H, as vowels are not indicated in Hebrew. In kabbalah, these three letters refer to the mystery of Pi, Tau, and He, which stands for "I am the circle and the cross." Here, the circle is God unmanifested and the cross is God manifested. When Jesus was in Gethsemane and the Roman soldiers came to seize Him, they asked Him if He was the Jesus of Nazareth, the Redeemer of the Jews, and He replied, "I am that." It is possible that He said it in a tone that caused all the soldiers to fall to the ground, unable to capture Him, as recounted by the Gospel. When they asked, "Are You that?" and He replied, "I am that." His tone implied, "I am God." After this, He instantly returned to being a personal human, and the soldiers seized Him.

I think it is psychologically peculiar how all the soldiers fell to the ground. It is not a common occurrence for detectives to fall to the ground when apprehending a criminal. It is usually the other way around. However, upon seizing Jesus Christ, the soldiers fell down to worship him.

Jesus Christ was thus the incarnate God, the love incarnate. We would not have been able to receive the image of God into our physical consciousness if Jesus Christ, the human being through which God and love were made incarnate, had not appeared on Earth. Now that He has appeared, we have seen God, and thus, we know the image of God; we know God in our physical consciousness. If God's love had not come here on Earth as a living being, we would not have had any certain knowledge of it. Consider your own psychology: Even if you have, in your imagination, understood ethics and grasped that you must aspire ethically towards goodness, you cannot pursue this aspiration further if you keep asking yourself, "Is this pursuit of good worth doing? How can one know that God is love and that the law of life requires us to be noble, good, and honest? How do I know all this?" Relying solely on our own reason is very flimsy. We humans always need a support; we need another human who can support our reason. Seeing a Master in the physical world gives us the foundation that lets us know that right there is a human being who has achieved perfection, who has become love incarnate. This memory, this knowledge supports us. However, if we lack such experience, we are always left more or less ignorant, even if our reason has studied as many religions as possible. Even if we comprehend all the great religions and teachers, we cannot, on our own, find the teacher, the great redeemer, who was a perfect human, who is of God, who is divine. There is only one of whom we can say nothing but good; there are no flaws in Him, no faults, no stains. He is Jesus Christ, God on Earth, love incarnate.

When we read the Gospel and understand that this person not only existed but still exists, we finally understand that no one is in distress any longer. We come to believe that we have been bought with a price and are all on the path to salvation. We all need a door, a "ptah", which we can find in another living person, and it is an absolutely perfect door. We may ask ourselves: have not the Christian churches always preached this exact thing? They have always taught it, yet in practice, they have consistently strayed from it. They did adopt the idea, but they turned it into dogma. This is not dogma. This knowledge comes to people only in great distress. This is not the kind of knowledge that can be obtained in school. When it becomes dogma, it turns into a travesty. By doing this, the churches proselytize the spirit of the Antichrist. The spirit of Antichrist is the denial of the teachings of Christ, as St. John wrote, "We call 'Lord, Lord!' but we do not fulfill his commandments and then he says to us, 'Go away from me, I do not know you. What does it help if you say that I am Lord and God, I do not need that. You must follow my commandments.'" People are following the spirit of Christ only when they are following His commandments, otherwise they travel in the spirit of the Antichrist. Has the Christian Church taken the commandments of Jesus Christ as their guiding line? No! Thus, they have become servants of the Antichrist. Jesus Christ does not hear the sects and churches that do not know or follow His commandments, no matter how much they call, "Lord, Lord!" We can say now, as we have said a thousand times before, "Christ is not a General but a Prince of Peace; those who follow Christ, renounce war, killing, and hate, and instead follow His commandments and teachings." But what have the churches done? They have limped along, not daring to accept Christ even if they have intuitively known and sensed the spirit of Christ, His doctrine. They have always given war their blessing, recognition, and support. They have not known of any better, thus setting themselves in the servitude of the Antichrist.

This is a clear definition of the Antichrist. However, we must never forget that a person, who only recognizes Jesus Christ as God, is not the Antichrist. One who, in their reason, only acknowledges Jesus Christ as God, is still partially living in the spirit of the Antichrist. A true Christian is one who follows Jesus Christ, lives by His commandments and advice, and attains the internal understanding and knowledge of Jesus Christ being God. This knowledge is attainable only by renouncing the spirit of the Antichrist and embracing Jesus Christ and His love. While this truth is known and understood by everyone, including the church, the error lies in our attempt to define love within our own soul and reason, rather than listening to the Master Himself. He says, "When you love one another the way I love you, that is true love." That is the sign of love, the love of Jesus Christ, the love of the Redeemer.

IX

How does Christ help us?

Spiritual love came to the world through Jesus Christ. This is what Western mystics and Rosicrucians assert, and it is indeed true. We can all acknowledge that it is true in the sense that through Jesus Christ, we can comprehend the spiritual love that encompasses all people and all living beings.

If we reflect on the times before Christ, considering, for example, the caste system of India, we see how it was impossible for individuals to understand universal love. The Pariahs were always excluded from all brotherhood, equality, and love. A Brahman, who was supposed to represent the wisdom of God, would abhor the Pariahs. He could not be near them. The Brahman ate alone for he was considered so pure that the presence of others with their impure personalities, or auras, would have contaminated his sanctity.

Turning our thoughts to Greece, we think of the grand philosopher – according to the Christian church, the Christian philosopher – Plato. Even he, the greatest idealist in philosophy, regards slavery as a completely natural thing. He thinks that no state without slaves can be the model state where order reigns.

When we consider these facts, it becomes evident that through His words, example, and life, Jesus Christ guided all people to comprehend the nature of love. True love, brotherly love, cannot exclude anyone from its circle, no matter how bad or strange they may be. However, this does not imply that the practice of true love was impossible before Christ, nor does it mean that everyone is currently practicing brotherly love. It simply means that brotherly love is now attainable for everyone. Everyone can now understand it better, whereas before Christ, it was not generally understood. Even to this day, we notice a great lack of love within those circles claiming to be Christian. For example, some American Christian priests, on their way to Palestine, had to travel a distance by a boat. They had already ordered their tickets, and all was set. They were supposed to visit the Holy Land, the Mount of Olives, and Golgotha. Suddenly, the priests noticed that they were joined by other Christian priests who happened to be black. The American priests immediately went back to the ticket office and said that there was no way they could travel with those black priests. Either the black priests had to give up the journey, or they had to take the next boat. The Americans arranged for the black priests to get their tickets refunded, and the black priests also received compensation for the delay in their travel. One can ask oneself whether those Christian priests really embarked on a pilgrimage. Did they truly go to Jerusalem, to the Mount of Olives, and to Golgotha to follow in the footsteps of Jesus, or did they go there merely as tourists? Their journey probably did not become a true pilgrimage, for right at the gate, they offended the first and last commandment of Jesus: the commandment to love.

Yet, they were all priests. As we can see, the fact that Jesus Christ brought spiritual love into the world does not mean that everyone would now practice love. It simply implies that we now possess a greater potential for love because we can now, better than ever before, comprehend the nature of spiritual love, true brotherly love. Love has always hidden in the human heart, but we must also admit that the work of Jesus Christ brought this love closer to the heart of every individual than it ever was before. This is both a mystical fact and an intellectual fact, and therefore we say that the life of Jesus Christ on Earth began a new age in the history of mankind.

How does this love awaken in us? How can we progress in our spiritual life? How can we get in touch with Jesus Christ? How, as an eternal being, a living force in our cosmos, does He help us? Where in our lives is He with us? How must we be for Jesus Christ to be with us, for us to truly feel Him, to truly experience His spirit? If we pose these questions, our task is to gain a clear understanding of this new era in the history of mankind and of these new possibilities. In these lectures, we have focused our attention on the problem of evil and have shown how we have been helped in understanding and overcoming it. While we have tried to describe the metaphysical help we have received, we have yet to touch on the individual lives, aspirations, and experiences of each human being. Therefore, our current task is to address these personal experiences.

I would like to emphasize that there is a significant difference between the aspirations of the current individuals and those who lived before Christ. Before Christ, when a private individual sought truth, spiritual experiences, or connection with the invisible world and God, their path always led to apostasy and renouncement. The individual had to give up their personality, essentially killing the self, renouncing it, and aspiring to unite with their Higher Self. This aspiration required leaving behind the personal self. The path clearly represented an inward aspiration towards the center and away from the periphery. The individual renounced the periphery, the circle, the sphere that was their outer self. They had to draw all their strength inward, fully turning their gaze away from this visible life and visible world. The individual had to die in the visible world to enter the inner world.

Once someone becomes a serious seeker of truth and God in the East, they often retreat from the visible life, choosing to live in the jungle as a hermit instead. There, the seeker meditates and gradually becomes aware of the world's problems, the great question of life. However, we rarely see seekers taking action as a result of achieving that enlightenment. Rarely, do we witness their return from the jungle to the world. Only the Buddha, having meditated and resolved the question of life and death, returned to the world to aid others. Zarathustra, Krishna, Laozi, some few have done so, but most seekers, the thousands, tens of thousands and millions of seekers of truth, have chosen to stay alone in their retreat. They have conducted their work from there, but they have only worked in the invisible world, as they, the highly evolved beings, have described, "We work in the world of thoughts and ideas. By meditating, we affect the thought-world of people." They show their love for mankind by wanting to further its spiritual evolution and to help it by sending out pure and beautiful thoughts to us human beings. However, we always yearn for something more immediate to us. We yearn for these evolved beings to act in the visible world; we yearn for their presence among people. Although only a few of them have returned to the world, this immediate presence is greatly evident in the personality of Jesus. He was no hermit or yogi retreating to some faraway place, working there in silence. Instead, He was a human who became a human among humans. He was perfect in His humanity, and thus, He was able to show us how we must resolve all of life's problems and how we can confront every part of life. The Buddha was similarly perfect, and his example is an eternal honor to him. However, we notice a difference between the Buddha and Christ, for Buddha suggested renouncing from life and striving for liberation from the cycle of life. He emphasized that existence is bad and miserable, and therefore advocated renunciation. Jesus Christ did not agree with the Buddha, stating instead, "The Kingdom of Heaven is at hand. The Kingdom of God is here in the midst of you, so you need not go to any jungles, you need not escape into monasteries. Instead, you must participate in life and actualize the Kingdom of Heaven in this life." This was the miraculous message and doctrine shown to us by Jesus Christ in His own life. He was the love which appears in servitude. The holy people of old, and those who still follow the old path, become almost worthy of worship. They embody such nobility that one feels compelled to kneel before them. They are so incredibly pure, noble, high, and wonderful. Jesus Christ, on the other hand, teaches that the one who is holy and pure and the first among you shall be your servant. Jesus Christ taught by His example that love comes forth through service rather than sanctity. A follower of Christ sitting on the highest throne of the kingdom, is not trying to draw attention to their own glory, but rather dedicating their life to serving others, to serving their nation.

In their example, the follower of Christ demonstrates that they have no other thoughts or motives in their mind than servitude. Jesus revealed to us this wonderful secret and hidden beauty of life. Only He has revealed it to us; no-one else has demonstrated it in the same way as Him. Therefore, after the life of Jesus, a new era began.

We can now reasonably ask: How can we participate in the life demonstrated to us by Christ? Without a doubt, everyone knows how it is done, and therefore the theory I am trying to present here is nothing strange to you, nothing new or unheard-of. It is only my attempt at trying to describe something which we all know in our heart.

I would like to say that in this life there are three waypoints, three periods or epochs, which occur more or less consecutively. However, these periods are not divided in a way, where an aspirant could not be experiencing the second period while still also going through the first one. Broadly speaking, the life of an aspirant is divided into these epochs or eras, but in practice, every epoch contains the powers and achievements of the others; they overlap with each other. The life of an individual, specifically their spiritual life, is now shown in a new light and in a new framework. It is now outlined in a new way. The life an individual lives before they receive the seal, traditionally referred to as the initiation, the great initiation, now serves as a preparatory phase in a significantly greater and richer sense than before. Prior to Christ, the preparation, or the so-called preparatory path of the aspirant, was shorter, easier, and more limited. However, it has since become longer, broader, and more human. These epochs I wish to talk about are part of this preparation. They overlap as they go, and they might also happen in a different order than the order I am now presenting. We also notice that this preparatory path is quite high and quite demanding. It asks much of us, yet it is only preparing us to join the explicit connection with Jesus Christ and to become his personal disciples.

These three epochs can be described in different ways, but I would like to differentiate them by our relationship to Jesus Christ in each of them: in the first epoch we comprehend Jesus the son of man and we believe in Jesus, in the second epoch we comprehend Christ the Son of God and we believe in Christ, and in the third epoch we comprehend God the Father, with whom Christ is one, and we believe in God. We could also say that in the first epoch we live in the aura of Jesus, in the second one in the aura of Christ, and in the third one in the aura of God, Lord God, in His aura, doxa, glory. During the following presentation we will also learn that in the first epoch we fight against Lucifer, in the second epoch we fight against Ahriman, and in the third epoch we fight against Satan.

We could briefly mention that these epochs also correspond to the temptations of Jesus in the wilderness, but because the temptations of Jesus, as belonging to Him personally, are of a totally different quality, they only correspond to these epochs if we adapt them metaphorically to our own experiences. Therefore, I do not want to talk about the temptations of Jesus in the wilderness this time.

When I say that in the first epoch we live in the aura of Jesus, believing in Jesus, I wish to add that this does not mean that we would have to expressly believe in the personality of Jesus, or even be aware of it. We do not necessarily have to know anything about Jesus in this first epoch, but we still receive the invisible influence of His personality, His aura. This occurs even if we had not heard anything about Jesus before this. We receive this influence even if we had grown up in the Eastern lands in different circumstances. We can still live in His aura and believe in Jesus, in what we metaphorically refer to as "Jesus".

This is part of the occult, psychological influence of Jesus on mankind, and it is more specifically part of the spiritual power that was emanated through Him into our mankind. This spiritual power includes the powers of the Buddha, the holy sages, the great redeemers, and the Secret Brotherhood. However, this power was brought closer to humanity by the work of Jesus Christ, and it now lives in our subconscious, in our soul. It might not appear clear and familiar to us in our daily consciousness, but it still comes forth from within us. Of course, this power is not the evil in our subconscious, which is a karmic result of our past. Instead, it is the power of good hidden within us; the power which rises to our daily consciousness and influences it.

The faith in Jesus, the act of living in the aura of Jesus, is now a precisely definable psychological phenomenon. What is this phenomenon like? It is the clear and aware knowledge and belief that our personality is important and valuable. We used to have to retreat from our personality, killing and displacing it, and aspire to attain the next level of unity with our Higher Self. However, this new faith Jesus is the belief in the preciousness of our personality, in its value and significance. The new faith is the total opposite of the previous understanding. We must no longer deny the value of our personality; we must not invalidate it. Instead, we must believe that it has a mission in life, for it holds a very specific purpose in this visible life.

How does this belief in personality appear? Does it appear as vanity? Do we become like peacocks, displaying our tails with their flashing colors? Does this belief imply that we see ourselves as extraordinary? No, quite the contrary. Vanity is wrongful behavior; it is the evil that sneaks into our personality alongside the good spiritual impulse. It is personal ambition and the exact opposite of living in the aura of Jesus. The proper way to emphasize and strengthen one's personality is very different from that kind of self-centered behavior: it is an act of liberation from all ambition and vanity. Lucifer tempts us toward peacock-like flamboyance, but living in the aura of Jesus Christ entails renouncing it. When one lives in His aura, it becomes apparent that pride, vanity, and generally speaking, ambition are not part of being human. A human being is not ambitious and proud. A human being is a worker, a servant of their own ideal, of their own truth. A human being is, if we wish to say so, a servant of truth. In the aura of Jesus, a human being emphasizes their own personality by believing in the divine goodness within them; the divine goodness which must come forth through their personality. This divine goodness cannot be imaginary, it cannot be wasted in the pursuit of illusory goals. Instead, it is expended through the lifework of a human being. When an individual gets to choose their own life's work, the work becomes beautiful, pure, true, and noble. As the individual expends the divine goodness in their efforts, the divine goodness in their life's work becomes apparent.

Therefore, this first epoch is solely about the work of an individual. Do your work in the right way. Firstly, as a youth, consider what your work and mission in life could be. Every artistic person and every exceptionally talented individual will have to face these questions: What is my mission in life? What kind of work should I pursue? These can be difficult questions to answer, but they are easy for those who already know what they want to pursue in life. Perhaps someone who is mechanically inclined wants to be an inventor. Their calling is the divine goodness manifesting within them. Someone else might feel that they were born to be a painter. They have painted and drawn since they were a small child. As a child, they drew in sand and on rocks with a piece of charcoal. They are always paying attention to everything beautiful around them. They see colors and lines in places where others see nothing. They feel that painting is their mission in life. When an individual lives in the aura of Jesus, they believe in their work and mission. This belief stems from their faith in Jesus, even if they lack knowledge about Him. Even if one lacks a clear supernatural mission, such as art, they still live in the aura of Jesus when they do their work – whatever it might be – as meticulously, conscientiously, happily, and perfectly as possible. Otherwise, they do not believe in that goodness and they are not faithful to their own mission and ideal, to their life's work. Someone who does not give all to their work is not faithful to their ideal. Dedication to work is a distinctive feature of those who live in the aura of Jesus.

We notice that those who try to be meticulous in their menial vocation or faithful in their life's work are somewhat oppressed by the life around them. They are faced with adversaries. For example, their own family might not understand them, even thinking that they are immoral. An individual who wants to become an artist, who knows their ideal and life's work from a young age, might face opposition from their family. The family oppresses the young artist, tries to thwart them by calling their work immoral and pointless,

"You cannot even support yourself with this line of work. It is absolutely wrong." The relatives try to come up with all kinds of opposing arguments. These are merely temptations the young artist must overcome. The artist has to remember the New Testament teaching that a man should listen to God rather than to men. The artist must not lend their ear to the temptations of others, when their own precious work and the divine goodness within them are at stake. It is this goodness that the young artist is tasked with bringing forth into the world through their work and actions. Even if one's lifework is something ordinary, one's goodness comes forth in the conscientious execution of this work. One should not focus on their personal comfort, relief, desire, and laziness. Rather, one should dedicate themselves fully to serving others, even if it means serving only one's worldly master. In the past, people were often faithful and admirably obliging, but these virtues may have declined in the current socialistic time of the past century. When one refuses to listen to the voices of temptation and tries to meticulously, unselfishly, and purely fulfill their task, the people surrounding them become offended. They become the tempters, saying, "You could be doing less; you do not have to be so meticulous." That spirit has now entered mankind, as proven by the countless embezzlements, robberies, murders, and the like. People no longer want to fulfill their work with absolute precision; they want to take shortcuts. They are not living in the aura of Jesus in the least. Living in His aura, living in this first epoch, entails working diligently and believing in one's own mission and the value of one's personality. If I become a robber, I renounce my personality, I renounce the preciousness of my personality. I want to enjoy myself like an animal for a moment, no matter what happens to me as a human being. We are not entitled to be like animals anymore, because we have already become human. With tremendous effort, nature has made us human beings. After countless efforts, God has made us human. Do we now suddenly renounce ourselves, demeaning ourselves lower than animals? Life in the aura of Jesus is an effort to become human, the Son of Man, striving to understand humanity and become fully human.

There is a lot of ignorance regarding this matter. Therefore, what Jesus said holds true: one's true enemies are their own family members. Family influences individuals both from outside and within. Thus, the family serves as a metaphor: one carries their family within them. Everything selfish and evil within one will naturally oppose their journey towards humanity. That was the first epoch.

One knows from experience that living in the aura of Jesus is sweet. Even if one is unaware that it is the aura of Jesus, living in His atmosphere remains sweet. I fulfill my duties and go beyond them; I am faithful to my work and mission. This line of thinking is sweet; it already embodies the kingdom of God; it embodies the intuitive sense of the kingdom of God. It is a battle against Lucifer, who wants us to be proud and to withdraw from life, advocating asceticism and renunciation of the world. "You are aspiring towards sanctity, are you not? Leave behind the filthy world, retreat to a mountaintop, and become pure and holy. Be proud and show everyone how great you are," thus speaks Lucifer, but the aura of Jesus speaks a different language, "Be faithful in little things, be humble, do not think that you are called to sit on a mountain top. Instead, go be amongst people and serve them."

Now we come to the second epoch. One can already be experiencing the second epoch while still going through the first one, but usually these epochs take place one after another. I differentiate between these different epochs because there are different essential aspects to the human being.

In the second epoch, the individual lives in the aura of Christ. They have already begun serving the divine goodness within them. They have been exceedingly faithful in small things and have fulfilled all their duties. The individual has been in every way blameless, a true Israelite, in whom there is no deceitfulness. Yet suddenly, they become exhausted. "What is all this? What do I live for? Why have I tried to be faithful, to fulfill my duties, to be as good and obliging as possible? I have tried to help others, but now I am ashamed: I see that I am absolutely nothing. What is all this? What is this whole existence for?" When one faces this tremendous fatigue, this great turning point in their life where they truly ask for truth, one becomes aware that even if they had been as good and exemplary, as righteous and obliging as possible, they might not yet have fulfilled their purpose in life. "Is there an even greater purpose in life? What if I have yet to learn the true nature of life, even after faithfully serving my ideal? Does God have a predestined plan for me to follow, a will for me to fulfill?"

When an individual starts asking these questions, some kind of change of mind and conversion occurs within them. The individual becomes weary of life, which leads to their conversion. Their mindset shifts, and they are reborn. They come to Christ, touching upon His aura. The individual acquires the intuition and feeling that there exists a unified life. The individual realizes that they must dedicate their personality to this unified life. They dedicate to it their strong, well-raised, well-developed personality, one that does not murder, steal, commit crime, or do evil. The individual has always dedicated their personality to the service of their own ideal, but now they realize that there is a great unified life behind all mankind calling them, "Give yourself to me." This unified life is Christ.

While still living in the aura of Jesus, the individual neither needed to feel devoid of sin nor strive to be exemplary, a perfect saint. Not a criminal by any means, they were still able to rejoice and enjoy life. The individual was able to commit small sins of emotion without feeling a sting in their conscience because they remained faithful to their work. This phenomenon is also demonstrated by great artists. They need not be living saintly lives, having never tasted wine, never eaten too much, or never made love. They are no saints, but they remain loyal to their work and ideal. A great writer once said that the main point is to be faithful to one's life's work. In this way, one does not have time to focus on improving one's personality or to judge oneself. It is as if even God would not judge those who are otherwise faithful.

Then comes this new phase, this new era, the epoch of Christ. Now the individual feels that there must exist something even higher. There is a greater life, a greater life's work, where it is not enough for the individual's spiritual self to be pure in its loyalty; their soul must also be pure. The individual starts to feel that their inner personality must now become absolutely pure and sinless. When the individual becomes in touch with Christ, even if they do not yet recognize Christ, they feel that they cannot gain knowledge of God's will without giving up on all that is selfish within them, without giving up their impure thoughts, feelings, and desires. This the individual feels as a seeker of truth. They feel that they cannot step before the truth and say, "Show yourself to me!" if they, at the same time, have other thoughts. The individual cannot face the truth if they cannot show the God of truth the thoughts and desires in their soul, if they feel that the face of the goddess Isis remains veiled from them as long as they cannot approach it with absolute purity. Every seeker of truth knows that the quest for the truth remains a mere game, a mere exercise, as long as they are not pure as crystal within, as long as they fail to embody the fire that consumes all their selfishness and evil. The seeker of truth knows this within. Therefore, the seeker knows that to attain the knowledge of God's will, the purpose of life, they must become completely purified.

At this point, the seeker of truth will also externally find the teachings of Jesus or some other Master or redeemer. Let us say that the seeker finds the teachings of Jesus Christ, and then within them awakens the belief in Christ, belief in the Son of God. They start to believe that Jesus Christ is the Son of God, the one who teaches about life and the will of life. A Buddhist may get the impression that the Buddha is the one who teaches them about life's will, but a Christian seeker living in the Christendom realizes that, for them, Jesus Christ can be the Son of God, the messenger of God, who teaches what to do and how to live.

The mission of the seeker of truth is to now begin following all the commandments, teachings, and advice of Jesus. Only by doing this can they go forward in Christ. The seeker enters the aura of Christ and lives in it by following Jesus, by following His commandments, His Sermon on the Mount, and all the advice of love presented in the Gospels.

Only that is true Christianity and true faith in Christ. That is the only way. Even if the seeker follows a different Master with all the power of their spirit and soul – be it the Buddha, Zoroaster, or someone else – they can still progress in the aura of Christ. However, the seeker must eventually also learn about Jesus Christ and His teachings. It is unlikely that even someone from the Eastern tradition, whether following the Buddha or some other wise one, would not encounter the teachings of Jesus. His teachings have been spread so widely throughout the world that they are available to all. They have sparked a lot of interest in the East. The Christians missionaries who have left to India, Tibet, and China, have thought that they are bringing the Christian Church to the Eastern lands. They will soon find that the Christian Church is futile, both in the West and the East. The Christian Church has had very little success in the West and will have even less success in the East. However, it is still important that Christian missionaries have spread the teachings of Jesus to the East, not by preaching dogma but by spreading the Gospel. Eastern people are beginning to intuit that Jesus Christ truly is the redeemer of the whole world. None of their own prophets have lived like He has lived. His teachings, His own words, and His Sermon on the Mount, have inspired and awakened Eastern people. A missionary once said that Eastern people do not yearn for organized church, for they organize and found their own churches, but they yearn for Christ, they yearn for His personality, they need it. They find what they seek in the Gospel and in the teachings of Jesus. Therefore, we need not belittle the aura of Christ, the doctrine of Jesus Christ. We can very well trust it: for the time being, it stands as the pinnacle of achievement on our planet.

We know that we can become true Christians and true helpers of the world by following the teachings of our own redeemer. The whole world needs these teachings. The mystical aura of Christ within mankind guides and reassures us, reminding us that we are not alone. When we travel in the footsteps of Jesus, live in the spirit of His love, and follow His commandments, we constantly sense the miraculous power in the air, supporting and helping us. We must be faithful; we cannot betray the teachings of Jesus or twist His commandments, but we must accept them as they are. When we accept His teachings, we overcome our soul, bringing joy to our spirit, and we find happiness. This is the battle against Ahriman, who blinds our soul, our inner sight, preventing us from seeing the truth. Ahriman causes us to veil the truth from ourselves by leading us to indulgence. Ahriman cannot enthrall our eyes when we follow the doctrine of Jesus, when we live in the aura of Christ, the aura of truth. In the aura of Christ we cease seeking for our own comfort. We no longer seek to satisfy our lusts and desires. We deem them all meaningless. We truly want our soul to be perfected and purified. We are already accustomed to being faithful to our own work and now we can become just as faithful to the inner work of our soul. We must notice that we cannot skip the lessons of the aura of Jesus: we cannot skip the first epoch even if we had begun our journey in the aura of Christ. We must also fulfill our lessons in the aura of Jesus. All lessons must be fulfilled, all must be created anew.

In the third epoch, we live in the aura of the Father. The third epoch is the battle against Satan. It entails overcoming Satan. This third epoch goes hand in hand with the two previous ones. It is the third epoch because we cannot fully delve into it until we have finished our duties in the previous ones. How can we live in the aura of the Father? Only by sacrifice. Sacrifice distinguishes this third epoch. The life of Jesus was sacrifice. He always lived in the spirit of the Father, saying, "– Not me, but Father." He was aware of the will and purpose of the Father. He sacrificed Himself, going so far as to die on the cross. Our life in the aura of the Father is also sacrifice. What is this sacrifice?

When Jesus was nailed to the cross, with the crown of thorns on His forehead and blood dripping from it, His back beaten so that blood seeped and dripped from it, and His hands and feet pierced with blood flowing from them, He refused to ingest the intoxicating substances offered to Him. No, He did not want them; He wanted to have a clear mind. No pills, no sedatives, no intoxicating drink that would render Him unaware of His suffering. He wanted to suffer with a clear mind all the way to the end. He wanted to sacrifice Himself. The cruel people standing around Him just watched as He was crucified between two thieves. How cruel and heartless! Despite knowing that this person had never sinned, never committed any wrongdoing or evil, and had only done good, those people still said, "He has helped others, but he cannot help himself." This is the secret of sacrifice. Those people unknowingly put into words the greatest secret of sacrifice. What sacrifice would it be if we were able to help ourselves, save ourselves? How could we then sacrifice ourselves? We can only help each other and save one another. That is true sacrifice. The sacrificial life entails going out to help one another, to save one another, even when no one is helping us. There lies the wonderful secret of sacrifice: embracing the sacrificial life saves us from all evil. If we understand to sacrifice ourselves by helping others, rather than prioritizing our own interests, we free ourselves from the power of Satan.

Let us imagine that an aspirant has a particular weakness or vice they are struggling with. They try to free themselves of that weakness by every method possible, but nothing helps: they cannot overcome themselves. The aspirant prays to Jesus Christ and turns to the Masters, crying out in agony. Yet, nothing helps their suffering; their evil is deeply rooted. What could offer them solace? Only going out to help others.

I had a friend in my youth – who has since passed – who deeply felt that he was thoroughly unclean and sinful before God, for he could not free himself of the allure of sexuality. He had an enormous attraction to women and he felt that even if he could externally control himself from indulging in sin, he would still feel unclean in his soul. He was always enthralled by the gracefulness of women. He constantly felt powerless before their sweetness. Then he received advice from Jesus Christ: "Sacrifice yourself: do not be afraid and sacrifice yourself!" I do not mean that Jesus appeared to him, but rather that he found this advice within the teachings of Jesus. This friend of mine then went to talk to prostitutes in different places. He taught them about human life and how they should free themselves from their situation. He even confessed to these women how flawed he was himself. Despite being unable to help himself, he still came to pray with them. Everywhere, this friend of mine faced real human beings. Right away, these women became human with him, revealing him their true selves. They had no desire for this life of sin. They had ended up in that life due to all kinds of reasons: perhaps they had been betrayed when they were young, and so forth. He did not meet anyone who had passionately wanted to become a prostitute. They all cried with him, and he felt that his unnatural attraction to the other sex melted away. Then he started to like one of the prostitutes, who already had a few children, and he asked her to be his wife. He liked her because to him she appeared so human. She could not believe her ears: "A real man, a real human being, without fault, who has never been accused of anything, who has never committed any evil, is asking me to marry him?" Of course, that was her complete salvation. They got married. They were happy in the truly highest and sweetest sense. When I first visited their home and heard their story, I cried, as I was still a young boy back then. His mission was his sacrifice: it was him renouncing himself, and living in the aura of God.

X

LOVE

At times, I have been asked, "Why do you, in your writings and speeches, always say that Jesus Christ means everything to you? Why do you assert that Jesus Christ is the primary redeemer of the world, and that His grace and beauty shines everywhere? Have you not, as a Theosophical scholar, concluded that all religions stem from the same source of origin, that they are all branches of the same tree? Does not a Theosophist believe that all religions are equally good and lead to truth? Humanity was not left alone to journey in darkness: God has always taken care of humans, as evidenced by the great proclaimers of religion throughout human history. These great redeemers have guided mankind towards God and truth. Do you not contradict this when you place Jesus Christ as the premier one, or even the only one?"

To this, I have answered that all religions have attempted to lead people to truth. They have all taught the truth about life and death. No religion has tried to lead people astray. All religions share the same objective in their metaphysical, philosophical, and occult teachings. They all agree with each other. When we delve into their inner, esoteric teachings, we find similarities in their explanations of the world, their doctrines, and their depictions of life and death. What do I then mean when I say that Jesus Christ means everything to me? I mean that the human soul yearns and thirsts for God; it longs for the living truth and the God who is the prime mover and source of all existence. The soul does not yearn for doctrine or any philosophical accounts of the composition and nature of the world or the cosmos. Instead, it yearns for the living God. "Like an elk thirsts for the water of brooks and lakes, so does the human soul long for You, God." It is the deepest yearning and longing of our soul. Only satisfying that yearning, by finding God, can we find happiness, peace, and eternal life. Therefore, all religions, as true as they are, differ from one another in some way. When they speak to people, they reveal God to them. Every great prophet or redeemer-being, wandering among people, has revealed to them God. Each prophet has given people a tangible picture of God, not only through their teachings, but also through their own persona, their being. These prophets and high redeemers have appeared throughout different times: initially in the distant past when humanity was less evolved, and subsequently throughout history as humanity has gradually progressed forward. Naturally, their descriptions of God have varied depending on nation, climate, and all sorts of things. If we study religions exoterically, without delving into their explanations of the world, but instead taking them as ethical phenomena reflected in their great redeemers, we acquire the image of God that these religions have conveyed to humanity. These images differ from one another, with most of them not being sufficient. None of those images of God imminently given by some redeemer-being has satisfied my inner yearning for truth like the image given by Jesus Christ.

Let us consider ancient Greece, with its Mount Olympus and pantheon of deities. The Greek god Zeus appears to us as a rather peculiar being who has all kinds of adventures in love. If we refrain from delving into the secrets of those symbols, instead viewing them as the means through which the God of truth announced Himself, we may find them distasteful from our moral and ethical standpoint. The god of the Jewish people, Jehovah, appears to us as a vindictive god prone to anger. Similarly, Moses, his prophet, became so upset that he smashed the stone tablets inscribed with the commandments. When we stand before these gods, we feel that none of them is the God we yearn for deep within. On the contrary, we feel that even a human being can, in love, goodness, forgiveness, and compassion, transcend such a god, who gets angry, avenges, and wishes ill for his enemies. We do not long for such gods; they do not satisfy our soul.

The noble story of the Greek Orpheus, a singer and musician, who ventured into the underworld to retrieve his beloved Eurydice, is touching and beautiful. However, Orpheus is not the God we long for in our heart, without whom we cannot find peace. Let us consider our Väinämöinen, the hero of Kalevala, who loves Aino and unsuccessfully asks her to marry him. His love for Aino is so beautiful, self-sacrificing, peaceful, and accepting, that Väinämöinen does not become mad or offended when he is rejected. He understands that this love is not meant for him. Still, he is not the God for whom our heart yearns. Our God does not appear in this manner.

Consider the gods and godly beings of India; for example, the old Rama, who is widely worshiped. He was a great warlord, and his spouse Sita was one of the most beautiful female beings throughout Indian history and mythology. These stories are beautiful; we can admire them, but neither Rama nor his spouse Sita embody the God we yearn for. Let us consider another Indian god, Krishna, who initially appears as a historical figure. The story of this young man is mesmerizing and touching; he demonstrates with his whole life that he is above all. Krishna, this divine man free of Karma, lived a seemingly frivolous life, filled with playful antics and mischief. For instance, he would steal the clothes of young ladies, who were bathing, and climb up a tree to watch their distress. However, he would eventually come down and spare the ladies from their difficult situation. We read about Krishna enchanting 16 000 gopis, wives of shepherds, so that they fell in love with him and danced around him. Krishna himself did not want anything from them, he only wanted to make their lives beautiful. When we read such stories about him, we understand how the Indians, burdened by life and yearning for liberation from the cycle of life, turned to Krishna, who was free from Karma. However, Krishna does not reveal us the God our soul yearns for.

We acknowledge that the more philosophical Krishna, as depicted in the Bhagavad-Gita, speaks wisely and truthfully in his peculiar conversations with Arjuna. However, we have to wonder about the part at the beginning of the Bhagavad-Gita where Khrisna incites Arjuna to war. When Arjuna asked, "Do I have to go to war against my own brothers? Is it not pointless to kill them all?" Krishna responded, "Do your duty. Your duty is to go to war. The killing of their bodies is inconsequential; they can be born again into new bodies. Do your duty in the service of the sword." We resonate with the Hindu who asked his friend, "Is Arjuna's stand not more human than that of Krishna's, who orders us to wage war? As a human being, Arjuna hesitates to commit acts of cruelty." His friend replied, "If this is so, then let us make Arjuna a better representation of God than Krishna."

The God brought forth by Krishna in that story is not the one our soul yearns for. Neither does Mohamed bring us the God we long for. We read how he took many wives, including orphans and widows, not for his own gain but to protect them. We have read a lot of good and beautiful things about him, but he does not bring us God.

Let us consider the Buddha, who stands as the highest of all human beings who have ever appeared on Earth, second only to Jesus Christ. He is the noblest of the noble, having renounced everything to seek the answers to all of life's questions. Yet, he also said that the only salvation lies in Nirvana. He taught that we must forsake all desire for existence and free ourselves from the cycle of reincarnation. Contemplating the Buddha leads our soul into pessimism, making us believe that there is nothing left but to renounce all, pick up a staff, and sit under a tree until we attain enlightenment, until we encounter God, who may be nonexistent or emptiness – the negation of all existence. There is no other way. However, I have felt from a young age that this God is not my God.

Therefore, I have chosen to follow Jesus Christ, who is completely different from all those other prophets and redeemers. Jesus Christ does not share their inhuman and undivine qualities. He embodies everything the human heart most profoundly yearns for; He is the perfect man. In His own persona, He brings God to people here on Earth as a new revelation and as a wonderful reality, saying, "Now you see the Father who is behind everything: you need not stumble in darkness. The Father and I are one; I bring God here to you." Who is this God then? This God is infinite, wonderful love. God is not merely Buddha's sympathy towards all who suffer, nor Krishna's aesthetic joy of the beauty of life; rather, God is love, goodness, and purity. He transcends all and resides within all. Our soul finds peace in the heart of God. Jesus Christ shows us the Father from whom we have all originated; the Father we can all find. He reveals us the Father who loves us, not with the love of young Krishna, not with the sympathy of the Buddha, but with a love beyond description. We must simply observe the example of Jesus Christ: how He loved, how He acted in every moment of His life, how He loved his disciples, and how He faced death. We must listen to what He said to the robber on the cross: "You, who have suffered so much, have been in such great agony, have experienced the hard struggles of life, have robbed, murdered, and stolen, come to me; today you shall be with me in Paradise." We must observe Him: how He forgave everyone, how He prayed for His enemies on the cross, and how He said: "Father, forgive them, for they do not know what they are doing."

This shows me the nature of God, and it is sufficient for me. We cannot understand the love of God, the love of the Father, the essence of Jesus Christ, or His infinitely sublime humanity, unless we have ourselves suffered. The more we experience agony, disappointment, difficulty, feelings of abandonment, and the sorrows of life, the more we understand and sense the love of God, the love of the Father. This the God revealed to us by Jesus Christ; the God whose incarnation He is. God was made incarnate in Krishna and the Buddha, God was brought forth by all the prophets of old and the sons of God. However, none of them could not reveal God to the mankind traveling under the illusions of ignorance, blinded by animalistic lust. Jesus Christ showed us God and brought the Father nearer to us in an unprecedented way when He fully embodied the Father within Himself, when Jesus of Nazareth embodied Christ, the perfect, heavenly man. The moment when the love behind all creation was physically revealed to all the living beings, humans and animals, was humanity's greatest moment of celebration and a wondrous moment for all life on this planet. Now we understand that only His heart has the rest and the peace we yearn for, and only His heart can resolve all our problems and questions. As awful and insignificant as we are, as sinful, incomplete, and criminal we are, when we open our heart to receive this light and love flowing from God the Father through Jesus Christ we find peace and salvation, become liberated, and truly transcend all our sordid states.

How does getting to know the gods of other religions liberate us from our evil will, selfishness, and sin? Studying different religions greatly supports us in our personal development and in our aspiration for overcoming evil. We find wonderful beings and magnificent people in all old religions. However, do any of the redeemers of those religions dare to say that they have found the living God? There are people earnestly seeking truth in India, China, and the East in general these days. Yet, those of us in the West lack understanding of their devotion, sincerity, and seriousness. They withdraw into the woods, and sit there for decades, struggling against themselves, rising to the highlands in their spirit. Let us consider all this. Perhaps they once similarly aspired in the monasteries here in the West. These wonderful human souls, who have aspired and striven, can agree with the hermit who sat in a small cave for 40 continuous years without going outside. When asked what he had achieved by sitting there, he responded, "I have achieved freedom from temptations." "So why have you not left the cave?" "If I had left the cave my soul could have been tempted by money or women. I want to be free of temptations, a master over myself." "So have you found God or eternal life?" "I do not know this, I cannot claim so. I seek and I believe that someday, perhaps after many incarnations, I will find Brahma." Is this not admirable and wonderful? Yet it ends with this: "I believe that after some incarnations I will find God, Brahma."

Do we here in the West understand how amazing and privileged our position is, for Jesus of Nazareth, Christos, taught us that God is love? God is not absent from this life, God must be brought into this life. We must not escape this world, but we must live here. We must make this world the kingdom of God and receive the love of God that is knocking at the door of our heart. We must live in His love. We must make our surroundings happy. We must all be faithful in the little things, until we are placed to preside over the great things. Life must be made precious; the life, which continues in death, if we attain eternal life. If we do not find God in this life, we can be reborn and try again. Why have we come here, if not to make something of this life? Why would we have come to this life if we just should aspire to leave it behind, as if it is not in itself valuable? The message of Jesus is this: "Your life is valuable; set it in the service of truth. No matter how simple or small you are, dedicate your life to the service of God. Love each other with the love I have loved you."

XI

LOVE ONE ANOTHER

In our everyday language, the word "love" rarely refers to the divine love or the brotherly love that religions talk about. Usually, we use this word to signify the expression of love, also known as sensual love. However, these terms "love" and "sensual love" are often used interchangeably. It would be beneficial to establish a distinction between these two concepts and reserve the term "love" for divine love, while using the term "sensual love" for the love that arises from sexuality. Sensual love serves as the first teacher for us human beings in all matters of love.

Sensual love is often spoken of with a hint of disdain and perceived to be inferior, particularly here in Christendom where it has become customary to regard sexual life as something shameful, not to be openly discussed. However, across cultures and throughout history, poets and those in good spirits have celebrated sensual love as particularly wondrous and beautiful. What would life be without this wonderful fascination with life born of sensual love? Surely, everyone has felt a new strength within themselves upon falling in love. It is as if one's soul awakens from slumber, emerging with newfound powers and abilities. Even if one did not possess a poetic imagination before, falling in love would certainly open their poetic vein. At the very least, they would learn to understand and appreciate poetry; they would become enthralled by a beautiful imagination. Love would color all their actions, and their soul would acquire a new base tone. A clairvoyant, observing someone in an enamored state of soul, can discern a difference between the person in love and others. This vibration surrounding the enamored individual is unspeakably beautiful compared to the auras of regular people. The aura of someone in love is beautiful, and it gives them a pure life. There is a feeling spurring them into unselfishness. The feeling spurs them to create something beautiful. This is visible in their aura, in the hues of color surrounding them. Therefore, the poets are not wrong but absolutely correct when they admire this sexual life and hold it as the highest allure and content of life. Of course, it is not asserted that sensual love is the highest form of love, but to those who have only experienced sensual love, it is. There are even higher ideals of life, higher forms of love. Every compassionate individual and seeker of truth takes a respectful stance towards this phenomenon, regarding it as an educator of humanity. They take a special stance, for with sensual love, comes a desire to help.

When artists, sculptors, and painters fall in love, they immediately feel a great creative power within them. Their poetic veins burst open, and they feel that they can now accomplish something. There are competent people, creative geniuses, who have wanted to live in a constant daze of sensual love. They are constantly looking for new objects for their sensual love because this falling in love, this sensual love and infatuation, does not last endlessly; it vanishes. It often disappears when there occurs a union between the sexes. That is when it usually disappears, but not always. Having lost this infatuation, the creative geniuses look for a new possibility to fall in love in order to gain new stimulus for their creative work. We are horrified by this. We deem it an immoral and sickly phenomenon when these great geniuses act like Casanova, flying from one flower to another. I do not wish to judge this phenomenon from an ethical point of view; I only emphasize the fact that this beautiful state of mind helps them create. Of course, ethically speaking, this aesthetic state of mind is bought at the price of other people becoming miserable. On the other hand, we must understand why gifted people often live like this. This sensual love is a marvelous incentive, a stimulant in one's emotional life, for a human is a being who cannot effortlessly receive inspiration from the invisible world. Inspiration can only be received when one's body becomes enveloped by strange vibrations through different experiences in life, such as sorrow, hardship, sickness, or love. These experiences can make a person vibrate. Every part of a poet's body can vibrate this way, allowing them to receive inspiration from above and create immortal masterpieces.

When we consider sensual love from a practical viewpoint and observe its phases in everyday life, we notice that in the context of marriage, a peculiar awakening occurs after two lovers are committed to each other: they suddenly realize they no longer fit together. The wonderful attraction between them vanishes and they feel naked like Adam and Eve in Paradise. They no longer understand the appeal of each other: "I should love that person but they are a total stranger to me; I see nothing in them." All kinds of little habits and attributes begin to bother them. Habits of behavior or thought, feelings, and requirements of life suddenly appear contradictory to them. Those two individuals who, in the ecstasy of sensual love, entered into marriage, now realize that they no longer love one another. They more or less lose their faith in love. They become cynics. As a result, we see these types of couples trying to get divorced. Divorce is becoming increasingly easier in certain countries, while others even legalize practices like polygamy. There are also marriages of another kind, in which both partners notice that they like one another more and more. They understand one another even though everyday life, with all of its ordinariness, surrounds them and the ecstasy of sensual love vanishes. They do not become unhappy by this; it is as though something new, something other than sensual love, grows within them. They begin to understand each other and think in the same way, becoming even closer, more familiar, and dearer to one another. Their life becomes happier, and their marriage more harmonious; their life is filled with new charm. Perhaps they do not immediately understand why everybody cannot be as happy as they are.

With all due reason, we may ask: why does marriage, in one instance, turn out to be so unhappy, and in another instance, so happy? To understand this, we must get a true understanding of what this sensual love is and what it is based on. Sensual love, or sexual love, is based on the magnetic attraction that draws two people together. What is this attraction based on? What causes it? This attraction is based on the differences between us humans; some are men, and others are women – opposites to one another. Thus, each one of them is only a half on their own, and only together do these halves form a whole. This is based on the law of complementing opposites: opposites complement each other. These opposites are akin to fractions in mathematics;

a man is one half, and a woman is one half, together forming a unity. A force of nature always draws fractions together to form a whole. As long as one is not complete but rather a fraction of a whole, one looks for another being to complete them. One seeks another who possesses what is missing in them, who complements them, and who attracts them, like a magnet. It is a rule in life that those who fit together form a whole, feeling magnetic attraction to each other. This law cannot be escaped. It is based on the fact that only a whole, in which the opposites are united, can create. An incomplete half cannot create. The perfect God cannot be incomplete; God is life that encompasses and encloses all, and the essential perfection of all creation. Therefore, God is eternally creative. Neither one of these opposites can manifest anything on its own. If the opposites are spirit and matter, consciousness and form, then spirit and consciousness remain completely infertile, incapable, and unproductive without matter and form. Form remains fruitless unless spirit enlivens it. Everything manifested is based on these opposites: spirit and matter. In God, in the divine life, these opposites are united as one. Therefore, the divine life is always creating.

Human beings are in a similar position; they are divine in that they can create. Humans are created to become creators. Naturally, this creation does not refer to procreation or giving birth, but rather to something higher, in a way similar to procreation but in a different form. This is why we say that great geniuses create immortal poems, paintings, or sculptures. In doing so, they have, in a sense, reproduced through their art; not through physical reproduction, but through true creation akin to divine creation. When one is destined to become a creator, a long process of evolution will take them to the point where they can create living beings like God. However, this does not mean that one would physically give birth. Physical reproduction is the way it is in the visible world because we are not whole, perfect humans, in the way our "Heavenly Father is perfect," as Jesus says, but halves of a whole being. Therefore, in this physical world two opposite halves are needed to form a whole. A man and a woman together, form a whole human being. Every child is a son of man, i.e., a child of a whole human. A child is neither the son of a wife nor the son of a husband, nor a "widow's son," a term used in the Old Testament. The term "widow's son" contains in itself a cry for help. There is something heavy and deficient in that term; it cries for help, for it is not the son of man but merely a widow's son. Every child is a son of man, and physically speaking this means that every human being is born of a complete human, that is, a father and a mother. At the same time, this aligns with Jesus' own understanding of Himself as the son of man, the son of Joseph and Mary who together form a whole human. He is their son, not someone else's. With the term "son of man," He consecrates all human sexual relations, which lead to childbirth. By childbirth, those relations have then become consecrated, as they have fulfilled their purpose in the physical nature. In this regard every child is also a son of man. Just as Jesus went from being a son of man to a son of God, so too is the potential and mystery of becoming a son of God hidden within every child. As Jesus Christ became the Son of God, anyone who is a son of man can also become a son of God.

When two married individuals, who are opposites that complement each other and together form a whole, become unhappy, they awaken to realize that they do not belong together. What causes this? No one can deny the great attraction that existed between them, so what could have caused them to no longer love each other? They did not meet one another on the level of love. Love is not depleted by sexual love, which in itself is a force of nature, a school of fate. Sexual love is caused by our imperfection, but this does not necessarily mean that we understand what love is. Two individuals who find themselves in this school may begin to introspect: why do I not love my partner? How should I love? If the couple has children, the children may be able to draw them back together. In this case, the couple reunites not out of love but for other reasons. Yet, they can learn to tolerate one another, to understand each other, and perhaps even love one another.

What about those who find themselves in a marriage by the command of fate? They naturally come to learn that they love each other. What is their love based on? It is based on a completely different matter; not on the complementary law of opposites, but on the law of union. True love arises from our similarity and unity with each other. Love is essentially just another name for friendship. Sexual love has served its purpose if it has led to friendship. We are mistaken if, as youths, we imagine that life is an eternal play of sexual love, or that we can always live in a constant daze of happiness. Such expectations inevitably lead to disappointment. Everyone who has held such beliefs has ultimately been disappointed. However, we can awaken to love and see God when we understand that love is the friendship between two human beings, and that true love cannot be based on any sense of incompleteness; it exists between individuals united in love — which is God. If we do not see God, then we sense God, we feel unity, and we recognize the similarity between each other, thus realizing that we have united with ourselves.

Love always comes through friendship and ultimately leads to Christ's love. Christ is the truth behind everything, uniting everything as one. True love — and there is nothing else but true love — is knowing Christ and living in Christ. Love is the connection we feel with each other. True love is not at all the same as the sexual love based on the magnetic attraction between opposites. Love is the friendship between spiritually complete individuals, the bond of brotherhood, and the complete surrender to one another. Love is living for others, as Jesus demonstrated in His own life and by His example. He loved, and those who became His disciples lived in a completely new, purified atmosphere of friendship and love. In this atmosphere, it was understood who God is and where the Father is, for Jesus could reveal to His disciples God the Father in every aspect of life. Therefore, Jesus is the only one who can completely reveal God to us, for His revelation is not only in His words — though it is certainly present in them too — but primarily in His being, His character, and His humanity. He is unique. He can teach us how we must be and how we must act in all aspects of life. We need never doubt again if we live in Christ. If we see Him before us and understand His advice and commandments, we can see Him in any situation imaginable, and we know how to act as human beings should, and we comprehend the will of God. It is no theater, but it is consistent in every possible situation on Earth. Jesus is our example, the God closest to us, the one who understands, helps, and loves us. We must embrace this great secret of love within our minds.

We must all understand that love is not based on opposites, but on union and friendship. Love is selflessness.

True love is akin to a mother's love, which is one of the most beautiful manifestations of love known to humanity. A mother completely forgets herself for her child; her love is unconditional. A mother will do anything for her child; she sacrifices herself and even faces death for her child. As St. Paul says, "All she suffers, all she forgives, and all she understands." A mother's love is a remarkable reflection of God's love. If anyone has ever questioned whether we can truly believe that God loves us when He allows us to suffer so much, then we can counter that by saying that therein manifests His ineffable love. In this school of suffering, we humans, who ourselves are divine, become aware of our own divinity, of our capacity to love. Here, we learn to love, for even if we knew everything, as St. Paul says, what would it be without love within us? This is a wonderful lesson in true love we are destined to learn. True love walks through strange paths. Sexual love aids us in taking our initial, hesitant steps towards love, and in the school of experience, we learn to love more deeply. We come to understand what love truly is, and we become increasingly filled with the spirit of God, which is the love of God.

When contemplating these matters, I comprehend the longstanding notion, particularly following the appearance of Jesus on Earth, that the life of Jesus, His message and His power should be disseminated by a special institution. All religions have established various forms of churches, congregations, and clergy, tasked with spreading their respective teachings. Considering Christ's message, His life, His life's work, and the gift He bestowed upon humanity, we understand the purpose and the mission entrusted to the Church and the clergy. This mission becomes clearer when we think of Jesus as a loving being, an exemplar, and a teacher guiding people on the path of love. Understanding this, we grasp the mission of the Church and the clergy. The Church was meant to interpret the message of Jesus Christ, serving as its voice, representative, and executor.

During the course of history, we have become accustomed to view the clergy with disdain. While we acknowledge their contributions, our focus often dwells on their shortcomings. As a result, we often conclude that everyone bears responsibility for their own spiritual journey. The Church and the priestly caste are based on the misconception that God is a stern and cruel God, who demands that His children behave. In the Roman Catholic Church, it is asserted that only the Pope holds the keys to Heaven: outside of the Church there is no salvation. Of course, the Church has a great mission: to let people into Heaven, individuals who might otherwise face hell and damnation. The Catholic Church believes it has a mission to remind people of God and the horrors of Hell, and to perform various tricks during events such as birth, death, and marriage to mend broken relations with God. However, such beliefs are just silly. There is no such God who would require an intermediary priest. Each individual reconciles with themselves and God only by rectifying the matters on their conscience and striving to live with a pure conscience.

Yet, when we understand that God is love and that He wants us to learn to love, we understand the potential of the Church and the clergy. As originally envisioned, they could have the pleasant duty of deeply understanding the commandments and teachings of Jesus, faithfully following them. They would know how we can find love, how we can learn to love, serving as exemplars of love. All priests would strive to love to the best of their ability; nothing more would be demanded of them. All priests would be required to love, otherwise they would not be followers of Jesus and proclaimers of Christ. If we imagine a caste of people who could love and teach love to others, who could follow the Five Commandments of Jesus and teach them to others, it becomes apparent that our Christendom needs them. Indeed, throughout history, there have been priests capable of love and well-versed in the life lessons of Jesus. They have earnestly tried to follow Christ. They have fulfilled a crucial role in humanity's history. No other role would be suitable for that special caste, other than being the exemplars of love and teaching others to love. Such a caste would never approve of war. The priestly caste would shout as the voice of Christianity to the nations and rulers who are losing their minds: "Remember who you are; remember you are human! As Christians, you are responsible for reconciling issues with love!" It would not be difficult for the governments and nations to resolve their issues with reason and goodwill, if there were a great number of people in each country guiding the evolutionary trajectory of humanity.

Such a Church and clergy would be marvelous. Working towards such a Church would be worthwhile. This is the direction we should be taking. This is a serious matter, but it does not mean that life should be serious in the sense that we must look sad and miserable, but rather in the sense that life should become more beautiful, more attractive than it has ever been before.

Regarding love, St. Paul wrote the beautiful, but often misinterpreted, words in his first letter to the Corinthians, the 13th chapter: "For now we see indistinctly, as in a mirror, as a riddle, but then we shall see face to face; now I know incompletely, but then I shall know perfectly, as I shall be perfectly known myself." It has been thought that these words refer to life after death, that we now see as in a mirror, but after death we see face to face. However, that is a misconception. St. Paul speaks of love. No matter how much wisdom we have or how much we prophesy, if we do not love, we can only see as in a mirror. Only when we love can we see each other face to face. Love opens our eyes, shows us the truth and allows us to perceive truth in all things. No matter how wise we may be, we see everything indistinctly, as in a mirror, and we are left to speculate about the things we cannot see. Only when love resides within us can we see things as they truly are; people as they are, and God as He is. Only the pure heart inhabited by love can perceive God and the truth. Therefore, everything in our life depends on love. When we learn to love others as Jesus Christ loved us, as He said, "Love one another with the love I have loved you" all the riddles will be solved, and we will see the truth and attain eternal life and peace and bliss.